## Pictures on the front cover
are from three dioramas made by Bjørn Jacobsen:

### The Cutlass Ramp Strike
A terrible accident on the carrier USS Hancock (May 1955).
Page 16-21

### Kurt Knispel, the greatest tank ace
Knispel engages three Soviet tanks in this diorama
Page 74-81

### F-100F "Misty" over North Vietnam
One of the "Misty" jets attack an NVA convoy on the Ho Chi Minh Trail in North Vietnam
Page 22-29

A tutorial for making military DIORAMAS and MODELS
© 2017 Bjørn Jacobsen
Independently published by Bjørn Jacobsen
Text, pictures and layout by Bjørn Jacobsen

ISBN-13: 978-1547075287
ISBN-10: 1547075287

# Introduction

I was born in Norway in 1942 and made my first scale model in 1957, 15 years old.
I was fascinated by the aircraft from the Second World War and used all my pocket money to buy all the model kits I could get hold of and spent hours glueing the kits together and painting them by hand.

At that time, there was nothing called airbrush, weathering, after- market products, photo etch, shading and all the stuff today's model builder uses and takes for granted. Neither was there any social media, where your proud work could be displayed for all to see – and be criticised—by people you don't know, and who certainly do not know you.

The only one to see your work back in the 50's and 60's was your friends and your family and they would say your models were great, and boost your self-esteem to new heights!

That was the happy time of modelling.

Today, the modelling is big business, and everything is very serious. Perhaps a little too serious.
The building of models and dioramas should be fun, fun and fun – not perfectionism.

After years of modelling, I find it more and more rewarding and challenging to make dioramas because it requires not only modelling skills but also a sense of realism and a lot of research and scratch building to get it as realistic as possible.

When I am building a model or a diorama, I always wonder:

What was the story behind the model or the incident I am trying to recreate?

Why was the aircraft or tank made?
Why did the incident take place?
Was it a success or a failure?

It gives me the opportunity to let the models tell their story – and a story, they always have.

It might seem difficult to build a realistic diorama, but I assure you, it is not difficult at all.

This book is about some of my dioramas and how I built them.

I will not go into details in the building, painting or weathering of the models, there are plenty of other publications which cover these areas.

The planning, the creativity and the implementation of all the different elements that go into a diorama are the main focus in this book.

There is no "right" and "wrong" when building a diorama, so if you disagree with me and the way I am building my dioramas, or want to do it differently, that's all right!
Don't let anybody tell you differently!

I like to photograph the models and dioramas and I try to have them look as lifelike as possible.
This is a way to record the models and dioramas that are a lot of fun and the results are often very rewarding.

I do not keep my dioramas. I either give them away or throw them away, but I keep all my pictures.

To share my work with the modelling world, I have my website

www.dioramas-and-models.com

which is visited by thousands of modelling enthusiasts.
I hope some of my models or dioramas might inspire some of you to give this exciting hobby a try.

Happy modelling!

*Bjørn Jacobsen*

## CONTENTS

|  |  |
|---|---|
| 6-11 | How to make a burning aircraft |
| 12-15 | Launching rockets and missiles from aircraft |
| 16-21 | The Cutlass Ramp Strike, July 1955 on USS Hancock |
| 22-29 | F-100F «MISTY» over North Vietnam |
| 30-37 | Operation Bodenplatte. The Luftwaffe's Last Hope |
| 38-43 | Day of the Typhoon |
| 44-49 | Blohm & Voss BV 222 the giant German flying boat |
| 50-55 | The destruction of BV 222 V2, Oct 45 |
| 56-62 | Battle of Midway, the story of the SBD Dauntless |
| 63-67 | The Battle of Taranto (Italy) 11 November 1940 |
| 68-73 | Hans-Ulrich Rudel, the best combat pilot ever! |
| 74-81 | Kurt Knispel, the greatest tank ace of all time |
| 82-85 | Kurt Knispel—King Tiger Commander |
| 86-91 | Katyusha, the fearsome Stalin Organ |

## CONTENTS

92-95    Launching the SA-2 Missile

96-99    The German Schnellboot S-100

100-105    Drama in Kattegat, May 1940 HMS SEAL and Ar 196

106-111    Blohm & Voss BV 138 at the Norwegian Arctic coast

112-115    Lysander, the famous SOE's "Spy-Taxi"

116-119    Hanna Reitsch, Hitler's female test pilot

120-121    My first diorama: Messerschmitt Bf 109 Crash

122-125    Ju88 Zerstörer Crashlanding

126-131    Bf 109 Crash landing in the Libyan Desert

132-139    B17 Flying Fortress Crash

140-141    Messerschmitt Bf109 E-7 Trop in Libya

142-147    Kanonenvogel Down

148-153    The Black Friday, 9 February 1945

154-157    Luftwaffe Graveyard

158-165    Photographing your model and useful tips

## How to make a burning aircraft

On the next pages, I will show you how I made the fires on a Heinkel He177 (scale 1/72) and an Arvo Lancaster (scale 1/48).
The He177 was a heavy German bomber with a lot of problems with the double engines in each nacelle. They had a nasty tendency to overheat, and the result was an engine fire.
The Lancaster was a British night bomber. The one I made was shot down by a German night fighter. You will see that neither of the aircraft I am showing here is placed on a stand. That's because I made these fires for picture taking, not as a part of a static display. There would not have been a problem to mount the aircraft on a stand, it was just not part of the project.
Many model builders have once made a burning aircraft, but many of them have no lights and a very dense smoke.
This might not be wrong, there might, of course, be just heavy smoke from a damaged engine, but many want a more dramatic fire with lots of burning oil and fuel, and that's what I have tried to do with these models.

# Smoke and lights

I have seen many attempts to build a burning aircraft, some look great, while many seem to have a problem with this. Many make the smoke too black and too "compact". If you use cotton to make the smoke, it is easy to make it thinner if you attach it to some kind of frame (steel wires or a cage of chicken wire). The cotton can be stretched as thin as you want, and it is not necessary to paint all of it heavy black, a grey or brown colour might also be good. If you have a problem with keeping the cotton in place, a good trick is to spray with ordinary hairspray to make it stiff. One time I used steel cotton to make the smoke. It turned out OK, but would probably not win any price for the smoke building. The other problem I see many have, is the light. If there is a visible fire, there should also be a light in there somewhere. The problem is that light produces heat, and heat might lead to a real fire.

You also have to think about ventilation and try to make as much free air around the light source as possible so hot air can be replaced by fresh air. The question you have to ask yourself is: For how long will I let the light burn at one time? If it's just for a short while, you might use a strong light that emits heat, for example, a halogen lamp. If you, on the other hand, want to put the lights on for some time, you have to choose a light source that produces less heat, for example, a LED lamp. You have always the option to put a regulator on the electrical input in order to reduce the light (and heat) when necessary. Of course, a battery operated light source is an alternative, but so far, I have not seen any that are strong enough to be used as a light source for a fire.

*For this Defiant, I used steel wool and painted it red to illustrate flames in the engine department. The result, in my opinion, was not very good.*

# Building the engine fire on the He177

The first I did was to remove the propeller blades on the starboard engine. These were, of course, feathered and had to be glued back later in a feathered position. Two holes were made in the nacelle to make space for two LED lamps (10W 12V). The electrical wires to the lamps went out on the underside of the nacelle and would be hidden by the smoke trailing the plane. I then cut some chicken wire and formed it as a base for the smoke from the engine. To add colour to the fire, I put some yellow and red cellophane under the wire. Then I used some white cotton, which I airbrushed with black/grey colour and attached it to the chicken wire. To stiffen the cotton, I used normal hairspray

*Holes for the LED lamps*

*LED lamps in place*

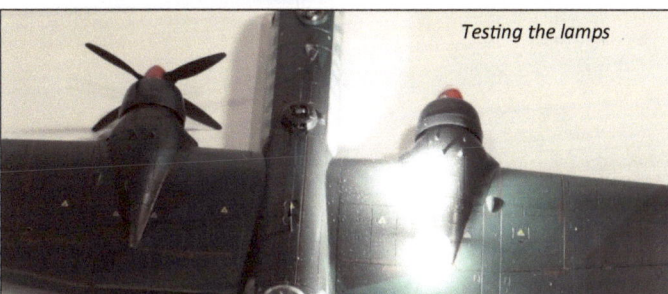
*Testing the lamps*

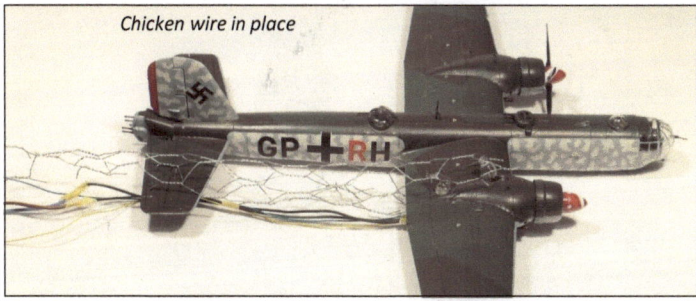
*Chicken wire in place*

*Cellophane inside the chicken wire.*
*Unpainted cotton ready to be fixed to the chicken wire*

*Cotton fixed to the cage and painted (airbrushed)*
*Wires are hidden inside the smoke. Lights on.*

# The Lancaster

To make the burning fuel from the starboard wing tanks, I needed several LED-lights (12V), colours and smoke. Before I made the big fire on the upper wing, I made some smaller holes in the under the wing and put a couple of small LED lamps into the wing. This would be the initial hits from the Bf110 which fired from underneath the bomber. On the upper starboard wing, I made a couple of holes to accommodate the lights. The flames from the fire would, of course, be blown backwards and I placed a couple of lights behind the wing. Chicken wires were used to support the smoke from the fire. The smoke was made of cotton which is very easy to attach to the chicken wires. Yellow cellophane inside the chicken wires was used to give colour to the fire. The electrical wires to the lights were hidden in the smoke. Last, the cotton was airbrushed with grey and black colour.

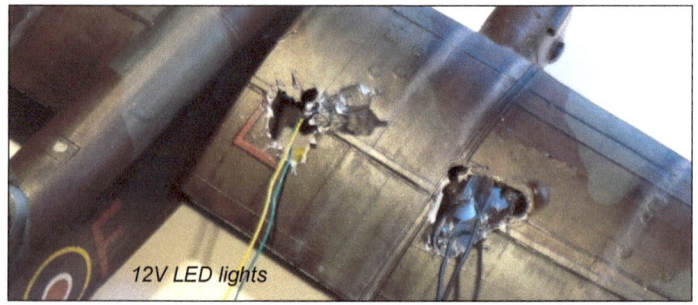
*12V LED lights*

*Testing the lights with cellophane*

*Chicken wire cage. Cellophane inside the cage*

*White cotton attached to the chicken wire*

*Testing the lights*

*Painting the cotton (airbrush)*

*The final result (the wires are hidden inside the smoke)*

Above: the Lancaster model (scale 1/48) on the base before the nocturnal encounter with the German night fighter (this picture belongs to another diorama).

The Messerschmitt Bf 110 G-4 night fighter manoeuvred by radar and manage to sneak undiscovered onto the bomber in the dark. From a blind place underneath the bomber, the Messerschmitt used its deadly 30mm cannons to destroy the bomber. The cannons pointed upwards and was called «Schräge Musik»

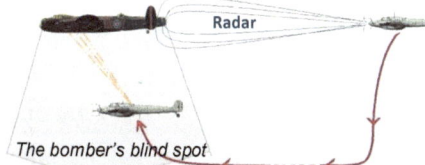

*Attack procedure of the bf110 Night Fighter using the "Schräge Musik" weapon*

I always try to picture the models in its right element. The Lancaster was a night bomber, operating in the dark and that made the photographing more difficult than normal. I placed the model on a stand and used very dark backgrounds. As in the real situation, the only light was from the fire. I turned off the lights in the room, turned on the lamps in the fire and took pictures. The Lancaster was attacked by a Bf110 night fighter. To complete the story of the Lancaster, I pasted a model of the German night fighter in the Lancaster pictures. Of course, that was not part of a diorama, but a part of the Lancaster story which I called "Deadly Nocturnal Encounter".
You can see more of this on the website www.dioramas-and-models.com (page 49, 50 and 51). More picture on the next page.

These pictures have been made by pasting the German night fighter in the Lancaster pictures. With the dark, painted background, it gives a reasonable authentic atmosphere.

These models are not part of a diorama, but it would not be very difficult to mount the aircraft on a rod, or tube, to make it a static display. The wires to the lamps can easily be hidden in the support rod. The problem, of course, is that with models in 1/48, it would be a rather large diorama. If anyone plan to do a diorama like this, I think 1/72 would be a better scale.

To the left: The bf110 (scale 1/48) is out hunting for British night bombers

Above: The last picture of the doomed Lancaster.
Below: The He177 «Greif» photographed in the air with the engine burning. Below to the left, you can see the actual photo line-up for this picture. It would not be difficult to place the burning aircraft on a stand in a diorama. On the picture of the He177 in the air, the stand has been removed by an editing program.
Below right: The He177 (1/72) on the airfield before take-off (this picture belongs to another diorama)

*The He177 quickly earned the nickname «Reichbrandfackel» (the Reich Torch)*

## Rockets launched from aircraft

If you are planning a diorama with a rocket launch from an aircraft, you might use the Katyusha method (see page 86-91), but you can also use the much simpler method which I used on a MiG-21 and a P-38 diorama. In the picture above, a North Vietnamese MiG launches two Atoll missiles against an American Phantom. The Atoll missiles were glued to the end of a thin brass rod and cotton was glued to the rod. The rod had different lengths and was fixed to the underwing pylons. It was important that the smoke from the rockets started behind the aircraft because of the speed. The smoke from the Atoll (a copy of the American Sidewinder) was almost white. The cotton was therefore very lightly sprayed with light grey colour and the fumes behind the missile were painted yellow.

The other diorama (below) is the "P-38 over Europe" where the aircraft launched a series of rockets on a German train somewhere in Europe. The rockets were glued to a thin brass rod, which again was covered in cotton to simulate the smoke trail. The brass rod was glued to the underwing rocket pylons.

*Photographing the MiG in flight and pasting the aircraft on a new background give a dramatic effect.*

# Afterburner on!
### (a LED light in the nozzle)

I wanted the MiG to be as realistic as possible and decided to have some light in the jet nozzle to create engine flames.
I used a 7W 12V halogen lamp which would not emit much heat, but still, give enough light.
The heat is always a problem with electrical lights in confined areas, and if you want to do something similar, please choose a low watt LED lamp if possible. It produces less heat that a halogen lamp.
Try to use 9V or 12V current. Avoid 110 or 220V.
But whatever you choose as a light source, only use it for short intervals, and never leave it burning unattended.

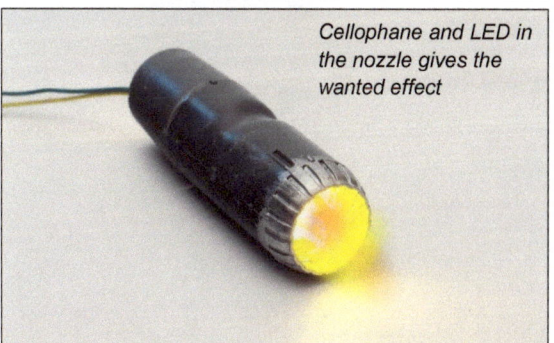

*Cellophane and LED in the nozzle gives the wanted effect*

13

## A couple of more pictures of rocket launching aircraft

In the picture above, I have pasted several items on the background to make the picture complete; (1) the train, (2) the explosion, (3) the aircraft braking away and (4) the main aircraft with the rockets.

On the pictures to the left and below, only the support stand has been removed.

Below:
A couple of examples of photographing the model - and the end result.

## The RF-4C shot down by the MiG-21's Atoll Missiles

*These pictures are part of a diorama/picture story of a true event during the Vietnam War. You can read all about the story on www.dioramas-and-models.com*

The explosion caused by the rocket was built around a chicken wire cage, fixed to the tail. Yellow cellophane was used to create some colour. Cotton was used to illustrate the explosion fumes.
Two 7W Halogen lamps (12V) were more than sufficient to make the explosion.
A large part of the Phantom's tail was blown off. Very thin metal sheets were glued to the holes in the tail to make the damage look authentic.

To finish the story, I made the ejection from the cockpit by the help of a LED light, a brass rod and some cotton. Because of the speed. the smoke from the ejection rockets trailed backwards from the cockpit.

The RF-4C did not start to burn, but it trailed smoke going down. This smoke was made with cotton glued to a rod and painted black.

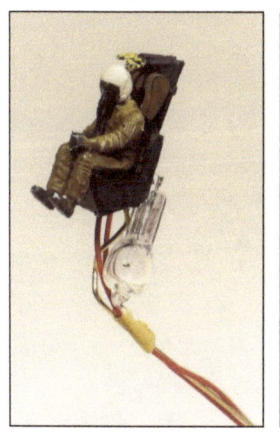 

*Small LED light glued to the seat and everything supported by a brass rod*

15

# The Cutlass Ramp Strike

This terrible accident happened on the 14 of July 1955 when a Cutlass crashed on the deck of the aircraft carrier USS Hancock
The F7U-3 piloted by LCDR Jay Alikir, USNR of VF-124 "Stingrays" was to land on the carrier.
The plane came in too low and insufficient motor power prevented the Cutlass from clearing the ramp. It struck the ramp and the airplane exploded while disintegrating airframe spins off portside.
The pilot was killed when the airframe sunk, still strapped in the ejection seat.
Note the LSO (Landing Signal Officer) – often called the Batsman or Paddles – running for his life. His name was Ted Reilly and - against all odds - he escaped the crash!
The hook spotter/talker jumped clear over the rail and was picked out of the sea later. The other LSO's leapt into the net and rolled away. Seven of the arresting gear people in the catwalk all escaped with minor injuries.

The dramatic pictures from the crash are the base for this diorama

# Chance Vought F7U Cutlass

This unorthodox twin jet carrier fighter had her first flight in September 1948. Unfortunately, the Cutlass had limited success and service, and a very bad safety record. The Cutlass soon gained many nicknames, the majority of which were very unsavoury, and for good reason. The "Praying Mantis", the "Gutless Cutlass" and the "Ensign Eliminator" were among the most popular ones, the latter owing to the high accident rate. Its loss rate was very bad. More than 25% of all Cutlasses were lost in accidents in its three years of service.

In the end, the F7U was deemed to be unsatisfactory for fleet use and was stricken from Naval Air inventory in 1957.

*To the right:*
*The 1:48 model used in the diorama*

# The Explosion

The model I used was a 1/48 model of the Cutlass which I had made before I prepared it for the crash.

The first I did was to rip off the wheels, the ailerons, the port external fuel tank and the aft part of the fuselage of the Cutlass.

It was clear that I would need a lot of lights if the explosion and fire should be believable.
I found several 220V LED lamps which I placed inside the broken fuselage and on the deck to create the explosion and the burning fuel.
The next step was to form some chicken wire to make a base for the smoke and fragments from the explosion.
The Cutlass had a high-speed skid along the edge of the carrier deck and the explosion/fire came both from the plane and the broken fuel tanks spraying the deck behind the aircraft.
I, therefore, made two "explosions" and used altogether eight LED lights to create the burning inferno.
Red and yellow cellophane was used to colour the fire and cotton was used to create the smoke.
I put cotton on the chicken wires and made sure there was as much air inside the chicken wire as possible (for venting the heat from the lamps).
The cotton was airbrushed with a small amount of colour (black/yellow/red) to help create the illusion of fire.

The wires from the LED lamps were hidden inside the cardboard deck.

Then I placed some fragments in the explosion fumes, among others, one of the jet engines which were ripped loose and seen flying in the air behind the aircraft on one of the black/white pictures.
The advantages of LED lights are that they do not get as hot as a halogen light.
There are a lot of battery-driven LED lights (flickering candle lights etc.) but all of them are too weak to provide the illusion of an explosion.
I had to use stronger lights and choose the 220V LED lamps (110V if that's your current)
Even if the heat from the lights was rather low, it gets hot after a while. The lights should therefore only be put on for a short time and always under supervision.
Just to be sure, I put a dimmer on the electrical wire so I could reduce the light (and heat) if necessary.

17

# The Carrier Deck

USS Hancock (CV/CVA-19) was one of 24 Essex-class aircraft carriers built during World War II for the United States Navy.
Hancock was modernised and recommissioned in the early 1950s as an attack carrier (CVA)
The Cutlass Ramp Strike happened on the port quarter and I had to make this part of the ship as a base for the diorama.
I used cardboard as building materials, which was easy to cut and glue together. The aft deck in the diorama measured 49 x 74 cm (20 x 30 in).
I had no exact details of the ship side of this part of the carrier, so I just used my imagination and some not-very-detailed-pictures to do the scratch building, thinking that the details of the carrier construction were not an essential part of the diorama. Besides, it would partly be covered in smoke, explosions and fragments anyway.
By glueing all kinds of stuff to the ship side, I thought it looked OK in the end (at least for a layman), even if none of the parts belonged to a ship.
The carrier deck, on the other hand, had to be a lot closer to the original. The USS Hancock had a wooden deck. The colour was blueish-grey with yellow markings.
Of course, there were a lot of stains on the deck from aircraft wheels and jet blasts. The arresting wires were very visible on the deck.

## Photographing the model with different backgrounds

*It's nothing wrong photographing the models on a shelf or on the workbench, but I like to place my models where they belong. For an aircraft, that is on the runway or in the air. To achieve this, I often have to use my photo editing program and paste the picture of the model on a more suitable background. Here is an example:*
*I "cut out" the model from its original photo and pasted it into another background. In this case, a picture of the carrier. I think this gives a lot more life to the model, and it enables me to "tell a story" by using different settings: The story of the Cutlass before it struck the carrier deck.*

# Here is my story of the Cutlass Ramp Strike:

*All the pictures on this page have been done with the same technique as described on the previous page*

## Heading for Disaster

The take-off from the carrier deck, the flight and the landing approach.

The plane comes in too low and insufficient motor power prevented the Cutlass from clearing the ramp.

Note the LSO (Landing Signal Officer) running for his life. His name was Ted Reilly and - against all odds - he escaped the crash!

# The Crash

If you want to know more about the tragic accident with the Cutlass, you can read about the story and see more pictures of the models at

**www.dioramas-and-models.com**

# F-100F «MISTY» over North Vietnam

In 1967, a group of combat-experienced fighter pilot volunteers were brought together in South Viet Nam to form a top-secret squadron with the famous call sign — MISTY. "Misty" was the radio call sign used by F-100F Fast Forward Air Controllers (Fast FACs) during the Vietnam War.

They were the 416 Tactical Fighter Squadron, and their mission was to fly the North American F-100F Super Sabre fast and low over enemy territory, armed with only their cannons and marking rockets… so low that they could see the targets… SAMs, AAA sites, trucks, bridges, troops, bulldozers… whatever.

Their goal was straightforward: Disrupt the transfer of enemy supplies and equipment down the Ho Chi Minh trail.

Misty's flew the two-seat version of the F-100 Super Sabre (nicknamed the "Hun").

The diorama shows a Misty attacking a convoy of North Vietnamese Army (NVA) trucks on the Ho Chi Minh Trail. The plane passed low over the column after releasing white phosphorous rockets and strafing the convoy with cannon fire. The Misty aircraft would only make one pass. A second low-level attack would be too dangerous because of the efficient North Vietnamese AA defence. After the first attack, the Misty would stay in the area directing Air Force and Navy fighter-bombers to finish the job – from a safe altitude.

# F-100F Super Sabre

I used a 1/72 scale F-100F. The first I did was to fix a metal rod into the aircraft so it could be placed above the ground. When the rod was in place, it was a straightforward process to build and paint the plane. The WP rocket pods on the outer pylons also had to be made because there was no such weapon in the kit. The Misty's carried no bombs, only the external fuel tanks; the rockets pod on the outer pylons and the 2x20mm machine guns below the air intake.

# North Vietnam Vehicles

Several different trucks, all in 1/72 and all of Soviet origin.
Looking at pictures from the war in Vietnam, I added camouflage nets which were used on the trucks.

The trucks carried both supplies and soldiers. One of the trucks was very near the explosion and was badly damaged by the blast. The figures are 1/72 North Vietnamese soldiers

# The Palm trees

The Palm trees were mostly made from scratch using wooden sticks and leaves I found in my back yard. The metal rod which was holding the Super Sabre had to be camouflaged as much as possible and I decided to make it look like one of the tall palm trees.
Most of the leaves I used were quite dry, and that was good because most of the lower blades on a palm tree is always dry and yellow/brown. The palm trunks were made of thin wooden sticks, covered with glue and sawdust to get an uneven surface.

23

# The Hut and the Peasants

I made a peasant hut to give more life to the diorama. The hut was made of cardboard, wooden spatulas and withered straws (which I collected outside my house).
The figures are 1/72 and mostly from Zvezda. Among the peasants were some carrying supplies and tending a horse.

# The Base

The base was a wooden plate size 90 x 55cm (35 x 22 inch)
The first I did was to draw the layout on the base; river, road and hill.

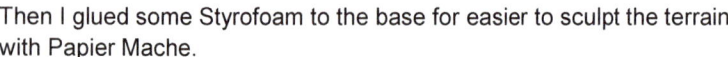

*The building of the house was perhaps not very sophisticated, but very cheap and in the end, it looked OK.*

Then I glued some Styrofoam to the base for easier to sculpt the terrain with Papier Mache.

The hillsides in Vietnam were heavily forested and I had to find a way to make trees and bushes instead of buying expensive artificial trees. I went out and picked what I found in nature.

In my experience, this will in most cases be more "natural" than what you can buy. Of course, the stuff I picked will turn brown in time, but a little paint will take care of that.

Another trick is to soak the leaves in Glycerine - and they will keep the green colour. An example: The reeds along the river are spikes from Barley (which are cultivated not far from my house)

The paper Mache took days to dry, and I used the time to put many of the trees in the still soft stuff, thinking I could paint the ground when it was dry. If you ever make something like this, do not be a smart guy like me: Wait until the paper Mache have dried, paint the ground and THEN place the trees or whatever you use as vegetation.

It was a heck of a job painting the ground with the "trees" already in place. A little artificial grass was used around the hut.

Altogether, I think I used 90% natural and 10% artificial vegetation.

The river was made «wet» by using a thin layer of Realistic Water (Woodland) on the painted river.

Around the blast zone, I made choppy water with Water Effects, also from Woodland

# The Explosion

I started with drilling a hole in the base for the electrical wires and decided to use 12V halogen lamps to create the explosion light. My guess was I would probably need 3 or 4 lamps to get enough light to make the explosion. After a little testing, I found that three lamps would be enough. Then it was the Chicken Wire cage.
The size was adjusted to the diorama and the dirt trail where the explosion occurred.
Of course, the heat from the lamps might be a problem, but the empty space around the lamps inside the chicken wires was satisfactory and the lamps would only be on for short times anyway.

**IMPORTANT:**
If you are building an explosion like this, never leave the lights on unattended!

This explosion should not be a ball-kind type of explosion. I have seen many explosions and my guess is that because of the White Phosphorous in the rockets, this will be an explosion with a lot of hot gases shooting off in all directions.

I, therefore, put some wires on the cage radiating out from the centre. The cotton could be placed on these to create the effect I was looking for.

After testing the lamps and putting some colour cellophane in the cage it was time for the cotton – as little as possible.

After everything was in place, I sprayed the cotton with hairspray to make it stiffen and used the airbrush to colour the smoke (the cotton)

I used as little colours as possible, the white colour should dominate, not black painted cotton.

At the base of the explosion, I used earth colour because of all the dust the explosion would produce.

Testing the lamps in the wire cage

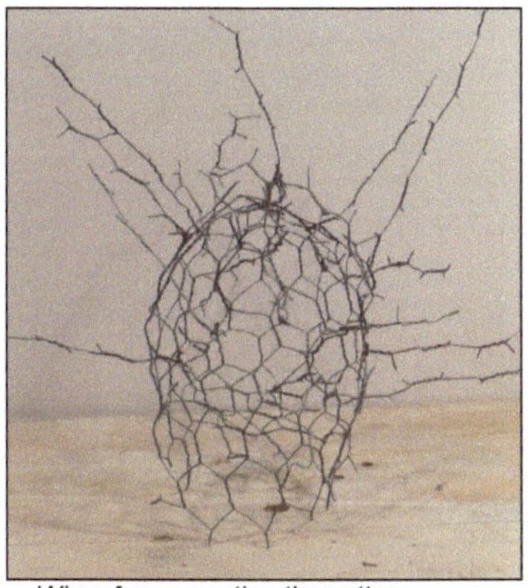

Wires for supporting the cotton

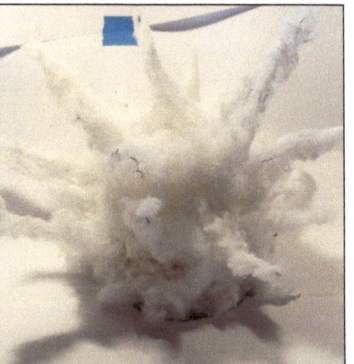
Adding cellophane and cotton to the cage

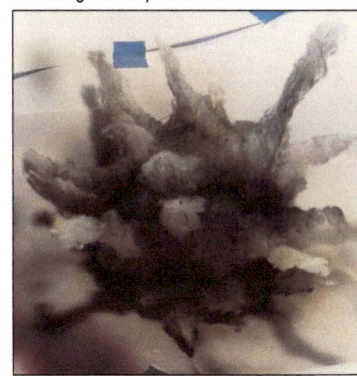
Placing the "explosion" on the diorama

Masking the explosion for airbrush.

The cotton is airbrushed

The explosion without lights

The explosion with the lights on

25

# The Background

The background was painted on a cardboard, hopefully giving an impression of the green, lush, forested mountains in Vietnam.
I studied pictures of the Vietnamese hills to make the background as realistic as possible.

## And this is the «Misty» diorama:

27

*The «Misty»-diorama*

29

# Operation Bodenplatte—Luftwaffe's Last Hope

It was the early morning of New Year's Day 1945 that Luftwaffe against all odds - and starved of fuel and fighting spirit - launched a massive, surprise, low-level strike attack on 17 Allied tactical airfields throughout France, Belgium and Holland.

The attack – codename Bodenplatte – was planned under great secrecy. The raid gambled on using the bulk of Luftwaffe fighter assets on the Western Front, with the aim of decimating significant elements of both the British 2nd RAF and the USAAF on the ground in Mainland Europe.

As the winter skies lightened on January 1st, 1945, more than 900 German aircraft, most of them Fw 190s and Bf 109s, swept across vulnerable and unsuspecting Allied airfields, creating havoc among the Allied planes ready for the day's mission.

A total of 495 Allied aircraft were damaged or destroyed in the attacks. Most of the targeted airfields remained out of action for up to two weeks. Fortunately, very few Allied pilots were lost.

The Luftwaffe lost 280 aircraft, 271 of which were fighters or fighter-bombers, with a further 69 aircraft damaged.

But more important: 213 German pilots were lost of which forty-five were regarded as experienced pilots and 21 were valuable formation leaders with skills that had taken years to acquire.

### For Luftwaffe, Bodenplatte was a total disaster

The JG 53's with their Bf 109s attacked Metz-Frescaty in France, the base of the US 365th Fighter Group. This was one of Luftwaffe's more successful attacks. The airfield at Metz was lined up with P-47D when the German aircraft attacked.

Wrecked P-47 Thunderbolts littered the field after the Bf 109 attack, but two days later, Metz was overflowing with factory fresh P-47s

## The initial attack of Bf109s from JG53 is the theme for this diorama

*Above: A picture from 1st January 1945, wrecked P-47 aircraft littered the field in Metz after the Bf 109 attack. Below: The finished diorama 45 x 85 cm (16 x 43 ins) Scale 1:48*

# Planning the diorama

Before I start building anything, I made a plan of how the diorama should be. Looking at pictures from the aftermath of the attack and studying the reports both from the German and American sides, I decided to show a Bf109 strafing the parked Thunderbolts. Three Jugs are placed on the airstrip as indicated on the sketch, parked wingtip to wingtip, all ready for the day's mission.

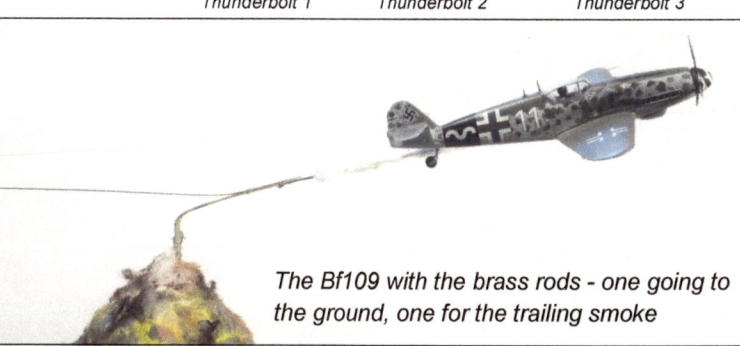

## The Bf109

The Messerschmitt was a Bf109 G-14 (scale 1:48) and painted the standard RLM74/75/76 with blotches of RLM74/75 and 70 on the fuselage sides. The spinner was black with a white spiral.

The German fighter needed to be placed in the air above the P-47s. What I did was to place a brass tube inside the explosion fumes from one of the Jugs and a brass rod extending from the port wing root of the Bf109. The rod from the Bf109 was then bent downwards and fitted into the vertical tube.

*The Bf109 with the brass rods - one going to the ground, one for the trailing smoke*

The Messerschmitt was damaged by AA fire (and later crashed) and trailing white smoke from an erupted cooling system. This smoke made of white cotton would camouflage the rod from the Bf109 to the ground.

The propeller on the Bf109 was a problem because it had to be "spinning"

*The cotton applied to the rods*

There are several solutions to this and I ended up with using steel wool (!). Three bits of steel wool were glued to the spinner where the propeller blades should be. Making the steel wool thinner towards the end and painting it in shades of black to off-white.

*The propeller blades made of steel*

## The Thunderbolts

I am using a couple of P-47 Thunderbolts which I build some time ago. The problem is of course that neither of these belongs to the 365th Fighter Group, so new markings and colours will make them look like one of the Fighter Squadrons parked on the Metz airstrip.

Pictures below: The "old" Thunderbolts (78thFG and 368thFG) to the left. The "new" 386th FS machine to the right (white noseband, white spinner and Code D5+)

I was planning on parking three Thunderbolts in the diorama and let the Bf 109 strafing go right through all three planes.

The first aircraft will be hit in the tail, the next in the middle section and the last in the front section.

The plane in the middle (#2) will be hit in the inboard fuel tanks and explode while #1 will have massive damages in the tail and #3 will be hit in the engine, explode and probably catching fire.

The planes will be parked much closer together than in real life because I do not have a 2m long base. Altogether, 22 Thunderbolts was destroyed and 11 was severely damaged by Bf109s on Metz-Frescaty airstrip on this New Year's Day.

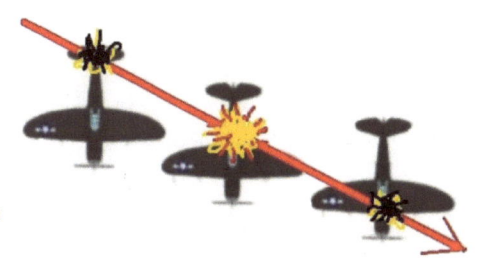

# Thunderbolt #1

The Jug #1 was a Razorback which was hit in the tail.

The tail was almost blown apart by the Messerschmitt's 30mm shells. Luckily there is nothing flammable in this part of the plane and the internal fuel tanks were not hit.
I use thin metal sheets to replace the thick plastic in the model, making the damaged part as realistic as possible.
In the diorama, we see the plane a few seconds after the rounds from the Bf109 hits the tail. The explosion from the 30mm round has therefore died and only smoke and shrapnel are left.
There will, of course, be visible damages on the ground, but that will be taken care of when I make the base

*Jug #1 being hit in the tail section*

# Thunderbolt #3

Thunderbolt #3 is hit in front of the starboard wing and fuselage.

I had to remove the front of the plane and cut out large pieces of the plastic to make room for the explosion in order to have as much air around the LED light as possible.
I also open up underneath the plane to make room for the wires and ventilation.

After the LED light is glued in place, I glued thin metal sheets around the openings to replace the thick plastic in the model.
I use a 4W /220V LED light.

30mm grenades are hitting the engine, blowing most of the cowling to pieces. The right wheel strut collapsed.
The smoke is just a thin layer of white cotton, sprayed with hairspray to stiffen.

Some shrapnels are glued to the cotton and last, but not least, the white cotton is airbrushed with a small amount of black and grey paint.

*Jug #3 being prepared for the hit.*

*Thin metal sheets glued to the damaged parts*

*LED lamp in place.*

*Cotton and fragments in place.*

## Please Note

*Light will always emit heat, also LED light. Not much from the lightbulb itself, but from the fundament that the LED is attached to. Please see that the ventilation around the LED light is good and don't let the light burn too long at a time.*

*The result*

# Thunderbolt #2

I had only two old models of the Thunderbolt, so obviously #2 is a new build.

This Jug was hit in the internal fuel tanks and blows up. The aircraft will not be built in a normal way because it will end up as a highly damaged aircraft.

The first I did was to cut the plane in two pieces to make room for the explosion.

To keep the halves together, metal bars were glued between the two parts and the LED light (3W/220V) was attached to the bars.

A cage of chicken wire was made to hold the explosion.

The vapour/smoke from the explosion should have a touch of colours, and some yellow and red cellophane were put inside the cage.

Besides that, there would be a lot of smoke, mostly black.
I was hoping that the use of cellophane meant that I do not have to use much airbrush colour on the cotton.
Spraying the cotton with several dark colours would prevent much of the light to get through.

It was, therefore, important to keep the colouring to the minimum.

Then I placed white cotton on the outside of the cage and used hairspray to stiffen it.
Now, it was time to place the Jug on the airfield and the cotton cage on the Jug.

The brass rod which would support the Messerschmitt was placed inside the explosion and glued to the base.

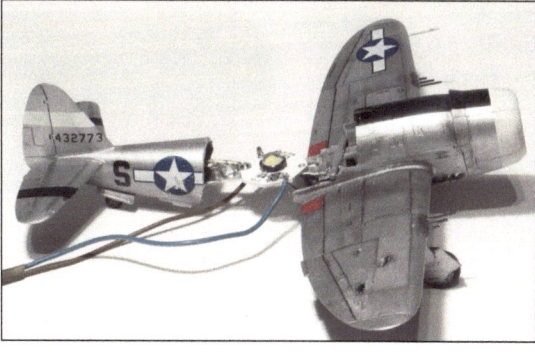

*The LED light is fixed to the metal bars between the fuselage halves. The electrical wires will go down under the aircraft and through a hole in the base. Cotton and cellophane are fixed to the chicken cage. Then the cage is placed over the aircraft and the LED light.*

*Above: cellophane and chicken wire*

*The painted cotton on the cage. Without light*

*To the left: The cotton on the cage before painted with airbrush*
*Below: With the LED light on*

33

## The Airstrip

The Bf109s attacked the Jugs on the Metz airfield again and again. The original plan was that each Bf109 should strafe the airfield three times and those who managed did just that – the whole attack lasted between 10 and 15 minutes. There was a lot of smoke, fires and debris, and I am therefore making marks and smoke where the 13mm and 30mm shells are hitting the ground around the three Thunderbolts.

## The Base and the Background

The base is a wooden board 40 x 85cm (16" x 34") which I painted on both sides to avoid bending when applying wet plaster on the surface. The base is partly covered by "Allied Airfield Covers" from Eduard and the whole area is partly covered with "snow" from Woodland. Pictures from Metz shows a snow-covered area, but only enough to show grass sticking up. In order to have a realistic background as possible, I decided to use one of the old photos from Metz airfield as a starting point for the background painting. The picture (to the right) shows the situation around the hangar and was taken shortly after the attack. AA-explosions filled the sky above the airstrip as all AAA-batteries opened up like crazy. The background is painted on a cardboard 100 x 60cm (40" x 24")

*Authentic photo*

Pictures (to the right) from the top:
    Shells hitting the diorama base.
    Photo of the airfield after the attack. Thunderbolts are burning.
    The base 40 x 85cm (16" x 34")
    The backdrop for the diorama painted on a cardboard

*The painted background*

## And here is the Bodenplatte Diorama:

The second Messerschmitt that you see in the background on the picture above is a small painting fixed to the backdrop

The background is 100x60cm (40"x24")

The brass rod that holds the Bf109 in the air is completely hidden in the smoke (cotton) trailing the aircraft.

Note also the smoke on the airstrip after the grenades that missed the Thunderbolts.

**If you want to learn more about this diorama and Operation Bodenplatte, please visit**

**www.dioramas-and-models.com**

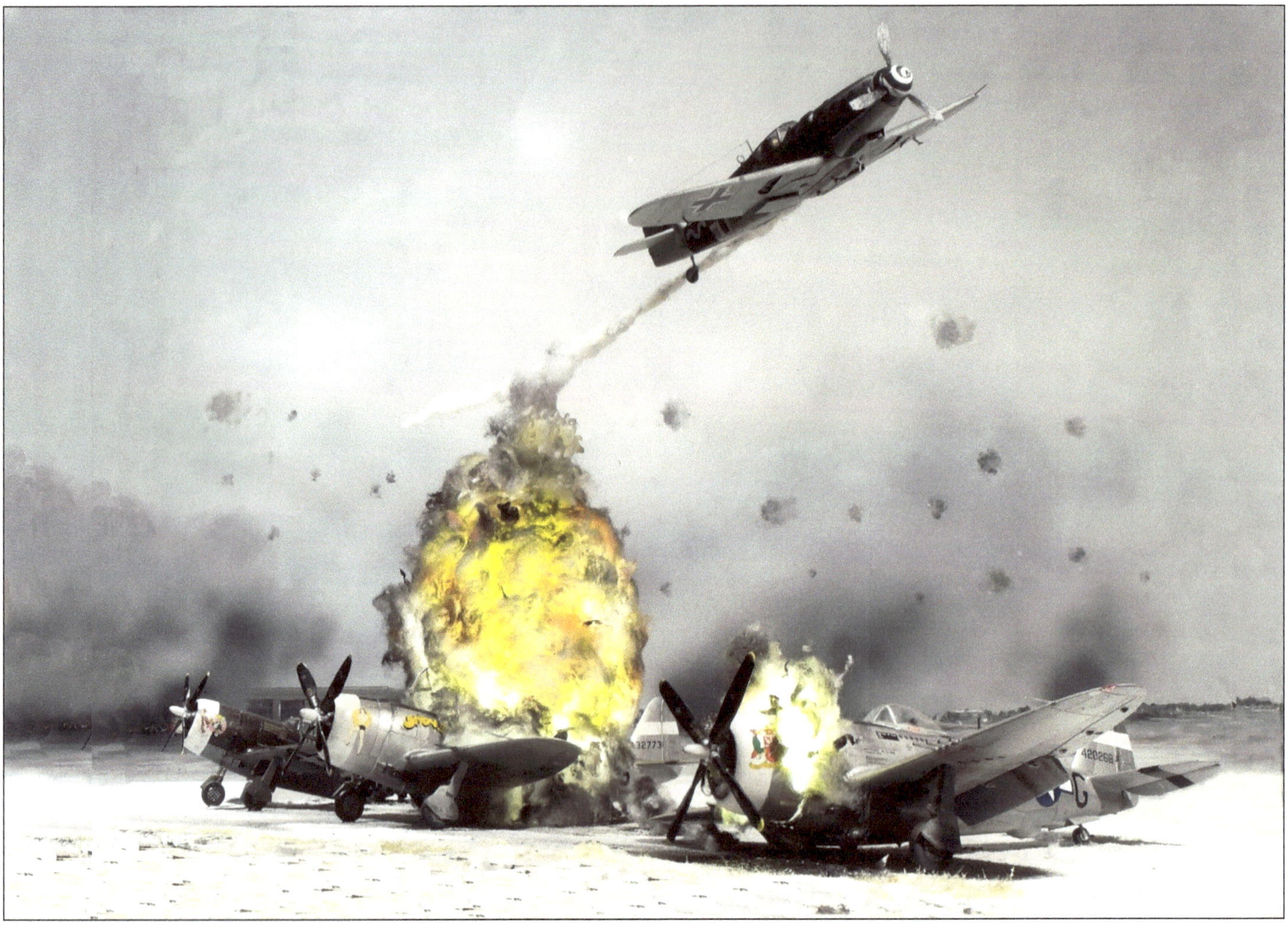

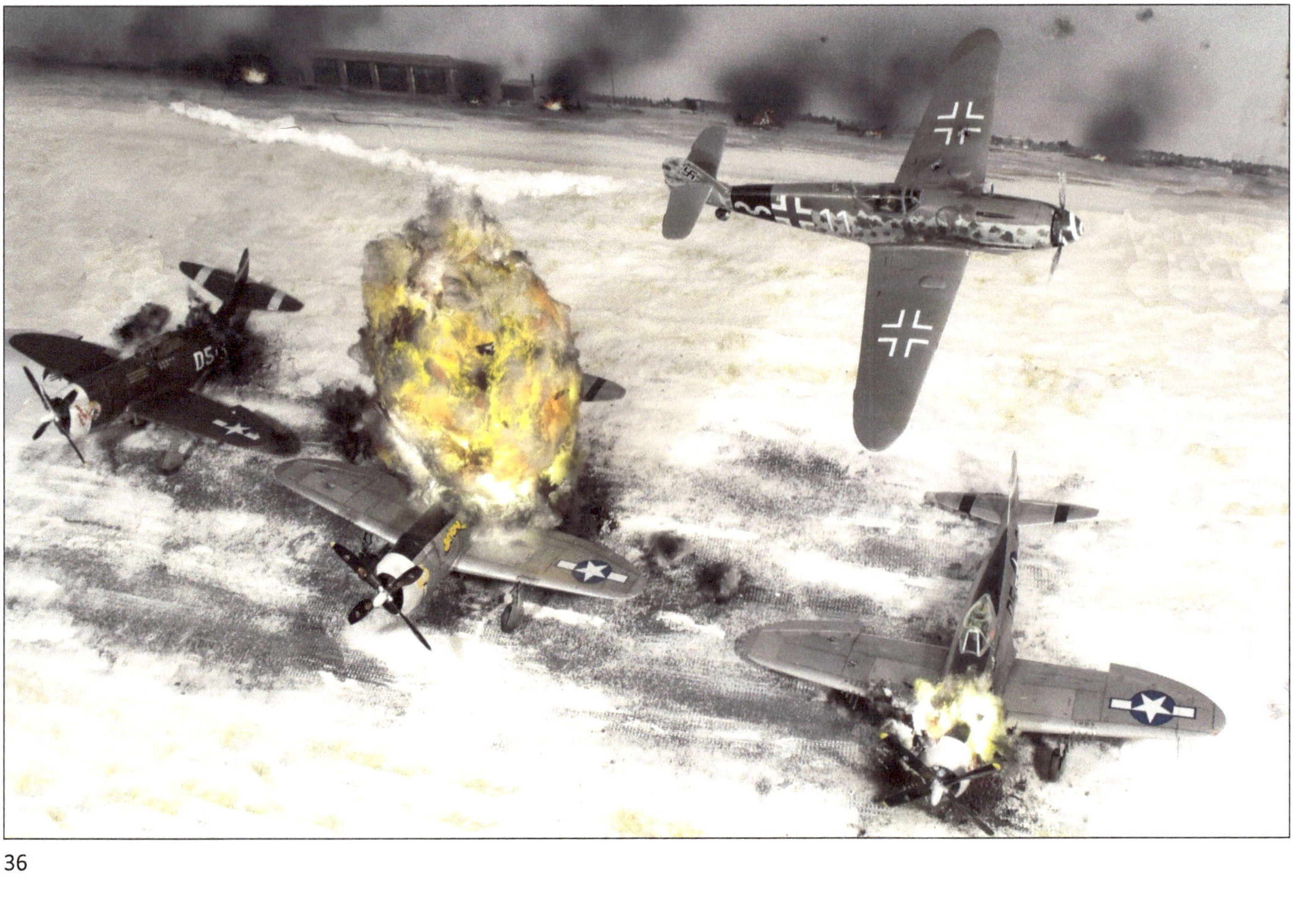

37

# Day of the Typhoon

Early in the morning of 7th August 1944, the German launched a full-scale counter attack around the city of Mortain in France. This was the first large-scale German counterattack after the Allied invasion. The main German force was the XLVII Panzer Corps, with one and a half SS Panzer Divisions and two Wehrmacht Panzer Divisions. Against this huge German force were only two US infantry divisions. By midday, the 7 August the 2nd SS Panzer Division had taken Mortain and the Wehrmacht's 2nd division threatened to cut off General Patton's US 3rd Army as it began moving into Brittany. The American had only fighter-bombers in the area and they were not effective against moving vehicles. Thus, the Americans asked the British 2nd TAF (Tactical Air Force) to send as many of their rocket-armed Typhoons to the area as possible. The Typhoons 20mm cannons proved very efficient in destroying soft-skinned vehicles and the rockets had a huge impact on the morale of the German soldiers, who were often seen to abandon their vehicles and scramble for cover in the surrounding woods when the Typhoons arrived. When darkness fell, the Typhoons had logged 305 sorties. One regiment of the 2nd Panzer Division was almost annihilated and the 1st and 2nd SS Panzer Divisions were seriously depleted.

## This was the day of the Typhoons!

*The German machinery (unpainted) which will be used in the diorama (the destroyed vehicles in the back row). 6 tanks, 4 soft-skins and 4 motorbikes*

## Building the Diorama

The diorama will show a couple of Typhoons attacking the German SS-division at Mortain.

To make it realistic, I needed a number of tanks and vehicles both intact and blown up and everything placed on a base looking like the wooden landscape around the town of Mortain. There would be a lot of elements involved and I, therefore, opted for 1:72 scale models to keep the diorama at a reasonable size.

Even if I tried to keep it small, the diorama was 73 x 50 cm (36 x 20 in)

The destroyed vehicles in the diorama are an Opel Blitz (Ffz 305 4x2) and an 8 ton Half Track (Sd. Ktz 7/1) with a Quadruple 20mm AA gun.
In the diorama, the Blitz has a 3,7cm Pak 36 anti-tank gun in tow.

The two styrene houses in ruins need some paint and scratch building to look more like real blown up houses.
More debris is put outside the houses when they are placed in the diorama.

The model to the right is an Opel (Sd.Kfz.3) Maultier ("Donkey") which was a semi caterpillar version of the Opel Blitz.

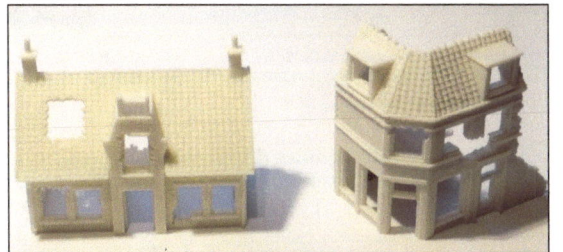

The German Tanks are three Tiger tanks (plus one exploding) and three Panzer III tanks.
The history buffs will know that there probably were no Tiger tanks involved in the Mortain attack.
The 2nd SS-Panzer Division used the Panther tanks. The only reason I used the Tiger was that I had them in my stash—and I did not think it made a big difference.

# The Base

I found a 73cm x 50cm (36"x20") wooden plate in my garage which seems to fit.

Before I started to mould the terrain, I made a sketch of what I was going to build.
I decided to have a small creek across the terrain. The roads are very narrow and levelled above the surrounding area.
There will also be trees and bushes.
The first I did was to glue Styrofoam sheet on the base to sculpt the terrain and then cover it with paper Mache.
Of course, the tanks will have no problem with crossing the creek, but most of the soft skins had to use the road.
The next step was to paint the base and make it ready for water in the creek, the trees and the bushes.
Additional painting will be applied throughout the build to make the diorama look right (scorch mark for explosions and burnings and so on)
Then I made (static) grass, added "Realistic Water" in the creek, put up the trees and bushes and made the village of ruined houses.

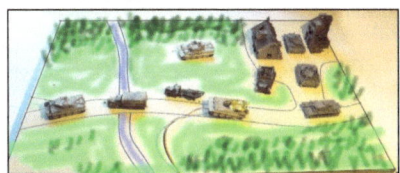

39

# The Exploding Tank

One of the Tiger tanks gets blown up after being hit in the engine department by a 60lb PR Rocket.

As a result, the tank tower is blown away.

The first thing I did was to cave open up the engine department and mounting a 25W halogen lamp at the bottom of the chassis. The advantage of a halogen lamp is that it's inexpensive and easy to get hold of.
The disadvantage is that the halogen lamps produce a lot of heat and you should be very careful if you chose to use one.

If possible, use LED instead.

I was thinking I could escape the problem if I only light the lamp for very short periods, but just in case, I also put a regulator on the cables to reduce the light (and heat).

Then I made the "bird cage" of chicken wire.
Before I glued the tank to the base, I drilled a hole in the base to let the electrical wire out underneath the diorama.

I placed the bird cage on top of the tank and put on as little cotton as possible (the less cotton, the more light) and made sure there was good ventilation inside the cage.

The cotton was painted (airbrush) with yellow, red and black. Then the chicken wires were fixed to the tank.

The explosion is caused by a rocket hit in the engine section behind the tower. This is the weak point of the tank, and it blows up.
The rockets trail a distinct vapour of white smoke. I want to include this smoke in the scenario.
A 0.8mm brass rod covered with white cotton will hopefully illustrate the rocket vapour.

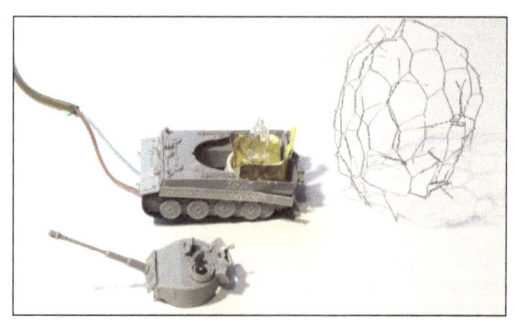

40

*The lamp placed inside the tank, Chicken cage outside,*

*Testing the lamp*

*The painted tank on the base. Lamp is visible.*

*Chicken cage placed on the tank*

*The cotton fixed the cage*

*The cotton is painted (airbrushed)*

*The light is on*

*The tank tower is fixed to the chicken cage*

## The Typhoons

The two Typhoons I am building for this diorama is 1:72 scale.

The models had to be fixed above the battlefield. There is no smoke which can disguise the fixture, so I had to settle for some kind of a rod between the planes and the ground.
I had the choice between a clear acrylic rod (8mm) and a brass rod (1,5mm).
I choose the brass rod because I believe this will be most invisible if painted in shades of green.
The brass rods are glued to the Typhoon's fuselage.
The aircraft is painted with camouflage, then with the black/white Invasion stripes and Duck Green tail band and spinner.

The propellers of the Typhoons should look like they are spinning.
There are many ways to do this.
I choose to use a thin strip of steel wool, which I painted in shade from black to white and glued on where the propeller blades should be.
This is an easy and inexpensive way to (hopefully) give expres-sion of a spinning propeller.

## The background

I painted a cardboard with the sky, some smoke and distance hills. I used a combination of airbrush and hand painting.

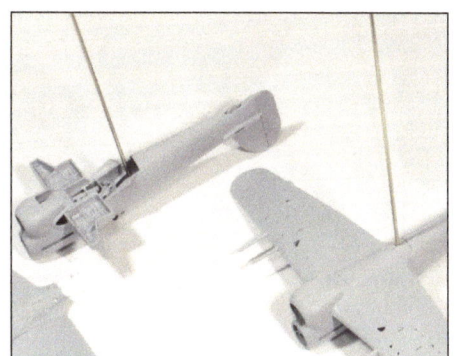

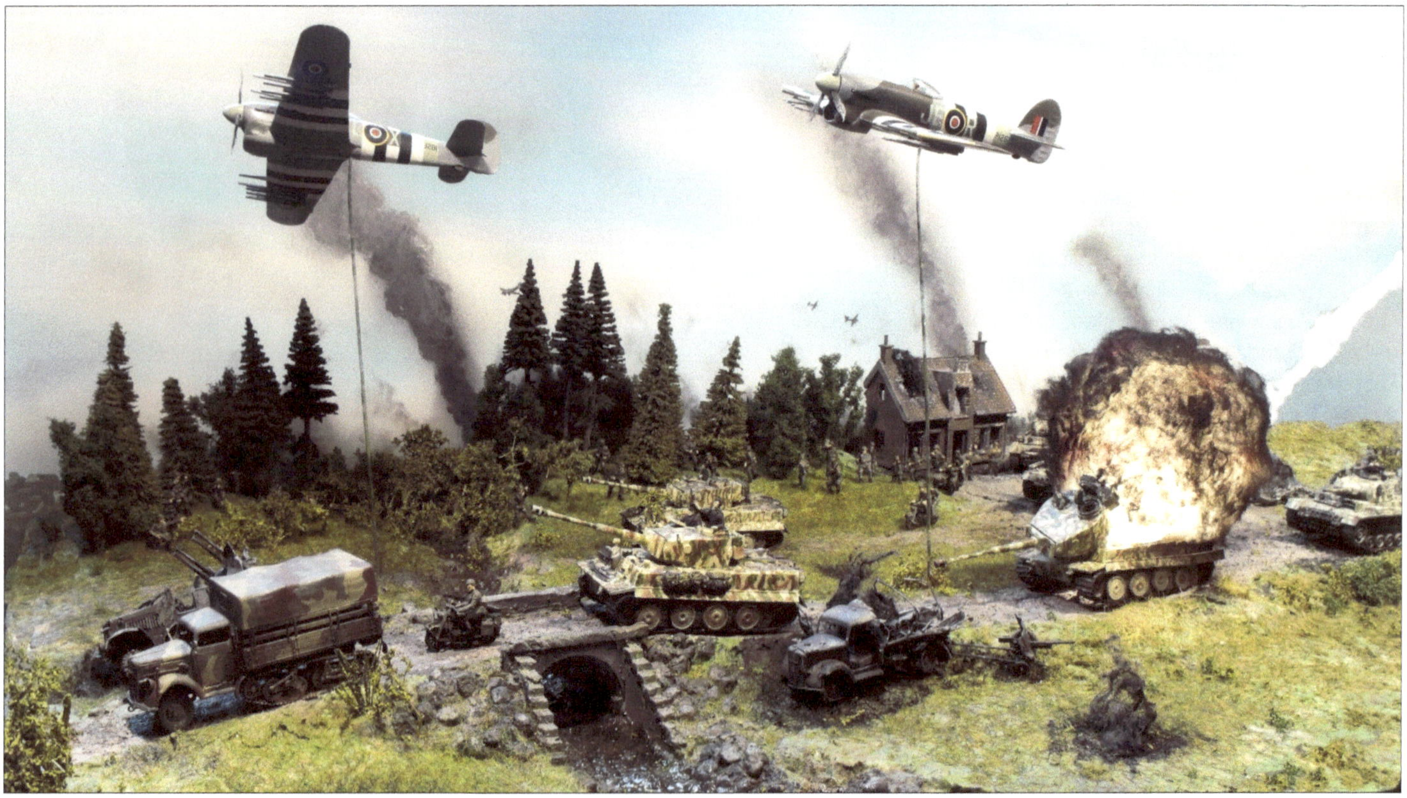

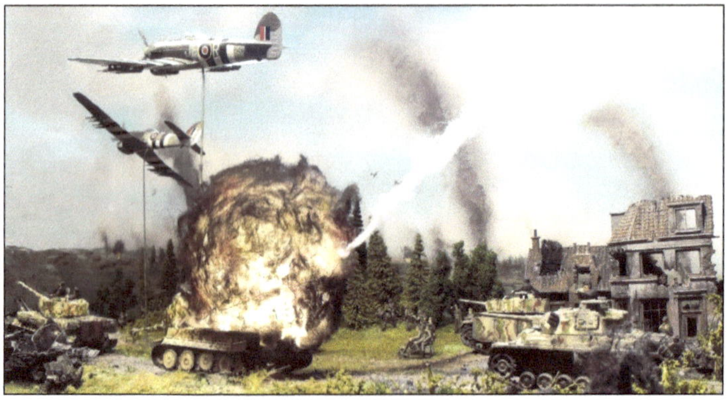

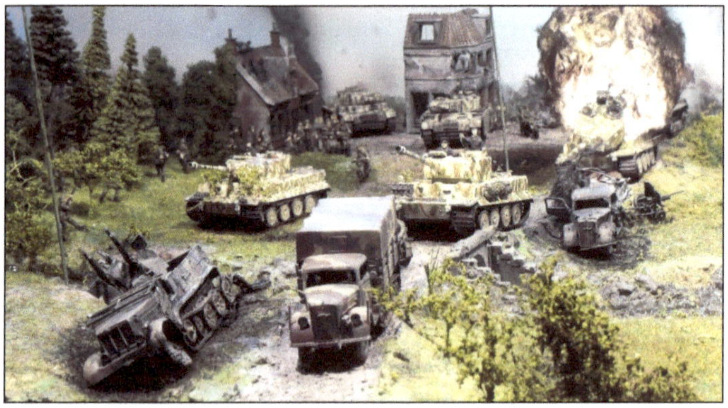

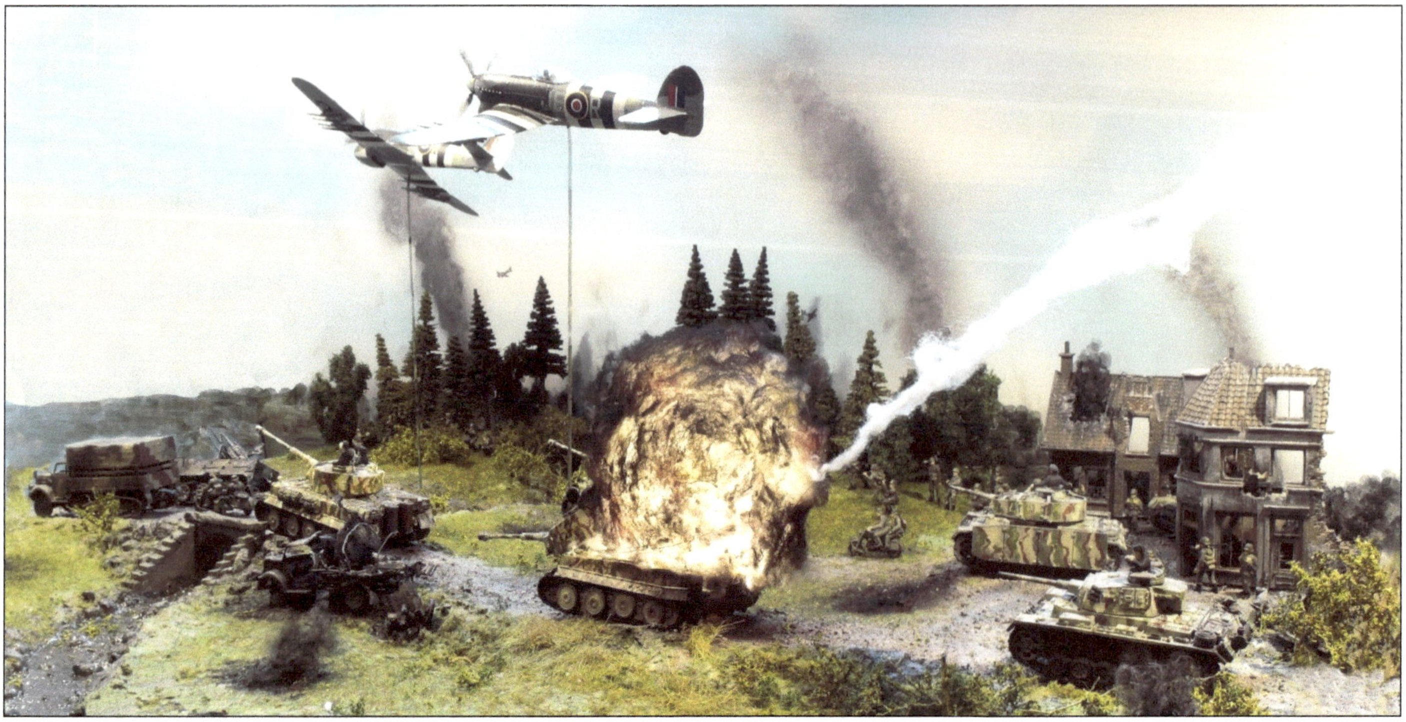

43

## Luftwaffe's Giant Flying Boat
# The Blohm & Voss BV 222 "Wiking"

The BV 222 was the largest flying boat to achieve production status during World War II. The six-engine Blohm & Voss Bv 222 Wiking (English: Viking) was designed as a passenger airliner for the North and South Atlantic routes but was taken over by Luftwaffe when the war broke out. A total of twelve BV 222 was built. The BV 222 could transport 92 fully equipped soldiers or 72 casualties on stretchers or 19.000 kg (42.000 lb) of freight. With a wing span of 46m (150ft), a length of 37m (121ft) and six engines with 1000hp each, it could reach a maximum speed of 390 km/t (242mi) at 5.000m (16.400ft) altitude and a range of 7.000 km (4.350mi).

The model I am building for the diorama is the second production aircraft, the BV 222 V2 (X4+BH).

It started its career in the Mediterranean, then moved to Biscarosse (France) where it got fitted with FuG 200 Radar, and then to the far north (Norway) where it stayed until the war ended.

The V2 was the only BV222 that was painted with winter camo. This was done in conjunction with Operation Schatzgräber (treasure-digger) to Alexandra Land in the Soviet Artic, July 1944. When the war ended, the V2 was in North Norway.

# Diorama Base

I used a 60x70cm (24x28in) wooden plate for the diorama.
The first I did was to sketch the layout with land, sea and aircraft.
The land was made of paper Mache and small pebbles, taking into consideration all the items that should be placed on the land (boathouse, landing place for vehicles, floating docks etc.)
Now comes the fun part: the painting of the water and the snow-covered arctic land.
For me, it is important that the diorama should look as close to the North Norwegian coast as possible.
The water was made by a layer of "Natural Water" from Woodland over the acrylic painted "sea".
The paint I used for the snow was matt and I had to use "Natural Water" to let it sparkle a little.

# Floating Docks and Boathouse

The BV 222 was a giant aircraft with the loading doors very close to the water line.
The difference between high and low water was so large that a permanent dock could not be used.
They, therefore, used a floating dock, which always had the same height above the water.
I made a couple of floating docks.
In practice, the docks would probably be much larger than what I made, but that might be as it is.
I also needed a scaffold for engine maintenance. This was made by styrene rods.
A boathouse is always to be seen in the North Norwegian fiords and I had to make one.

# Vehicles, Boats, Men

I chose to make a fuel servicing truck which fuelled the BV 222 and a Steur 1500 cargo truck which is handling freight and supplies.
The men are from different kits and the transport goods are mostly scratch built.
The rowboats and the launch are kits from CMK
The shed and the arrangement with the fuel hose are made from scratch.

# Different Backgrounds

I painted a typical North Norwegian coast landscape on a cardboard and used it as a background for the diorama.
When photographing the BV 222 in the air, I took pictures of the flying boat supported by a stand.
The spinning propeller was done with help of a photo editing program. Then I pasted some of the pictures of the BV 222 on different backdrops to create a feeling of the BV 222 in the air. You can see some of them on the next pages.

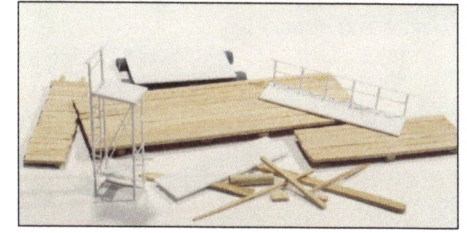

# Building the BV 222

The BV222 is the 1/72 kit from Revell. The flying boat was huge, so also in 1/72, 50cm (20in) long and a wing span of 63cm (25in).

The camouflage was the standard for all seaplanes in Luftwaffe (RLM72/73/65)

When the Germans painted the white winter camo in 1944 on this particular plane, they only painted the fuselage and not the upper wings.

This is rather strange because the upper wings are the largest visible part of the aircraft seen from above, and for the arctic trip to Alexandria Land, you should expect it to be camouflaged.

The reason for not painting white camouflage on the upper wings was probably lack of time. The BV222 was rushed to the rescue operation at Alexandria Land in the arctic.

Unfortunately, most of the model builders do this wrong: They paint the whole aircraft in white winter camouflage.

I have painted the BV222 V2 both before and after the winter camo was applied.

# Placing the BV 222 on the water

After taking pictures of the aircraft "flying" in the air, it was time to land it on the water.

I could have made a hole in the base for the flying boat, but this is always difficult, especially if you decide to move the aircraft to another part of the base. I decided to cut off the underwater hull instead. It was just a matter of taking the saw to the model and cut it off.

When the underwater hull was removed, the giant aircraft could settle down on the water.

# Photographing the aircraft in the air

With the help of a photo editing program, the picture of the model is pasted on a suitable background. The picture below is a good example of this procedure. The result: the model in its right element!

*The model is "cut out" of the picture of workbench-picture and pasted on a brand new background.*
*The result: a beautiful picture of the plane in the air.*

*To make the pictures to the right, the picture of the model is «cut out» and pasted to a new background*

47

48

49

## The end of BV 222 V2
This diorama is a continuation of the BV222 V2 diorama in the previous pages.

Two BV 222, (V2 and C12), were in Norway when the war ended. The British took the C12 and U.S. took the V2. British and U.S. personnel tested both aircraft in the summer of 1945. The Americans left V2 in Trondheim (Norway) in late August 1945 and in October; it was towed out in the fjord and blown to pieces.

### This is the background for this diorama

**The markings and painting on the BV222 in 1945 needs some explanation:**

The V2 (X4+BH) was the only BV 222 with winter camo. It was painted in a rush when the V2 was ordered to North Norway to take part of operation "Schatzgräber" in 1944. Only the fuselage was painted (probably due to lack of time).
When the British seized the V2 in May 1945, the Germans had just removed the winter camo (by pressure washer). The stains after the pressure washer are clearly visible. That is why the painting of the aircraft looks a little strange. The British overpainted the German markings and applied RAF roundels instead. For some reason, they painted the "wrong" roundels on the upper wings, probably because these made it easier to identify the aircraft from above. When the Americans arrived in August 45, they did not do anything with the roundels but instead painted a large American flag on the aircraft to show who owned the big flying boat.

*The picture to right was taken in Trondheim (Norway) in August 45, three months after the war by personnel from the U.S. Naval Air Center. It shows German pilots and maintenance personnel who helped the Americans in their tests. The guys in "civilians" are maintenance crew.*
*Just for fun, I coloured and pasted the old b/w picture to the picture of the model above.*

Before we start tearing the aircraft apart to make the final explosion, it's always nice to see the plane in the air. In this case: The American test flights in August 1945

These pictures were made by the help of a photo editing program:
A picture of the model was "cut out" from its original picture and pasted into another picture (background), creating a new and more exciting picture of the model in the air.

## Blowing up the BV 222 V2

I have tried to recap the moment the V2 was destroyed  It is not known how the British sunk the V2, maybe they just made holes in the bottom, but I believe that the BV 222 deserved to go with a bang, and decided to blow it up (which I believed the British did because the wreck of the V2 has never been found). To make the explosion, I cut some big holes in the fuselage; chicken wire and cotton were used to form the explosion fumes.  The cotton was sprayed with a grey colour (airbrush). To make the cotton stiff, I used hairspray. Two 3W/220V LED lights and three 10W/12V halogens were used to make the explosion. The wires going through a hole in the base. Yellow and red cellophane was used to create some colour.  Thin metal sheets were used to make bits of the fuselage and flying shrapnel. The sea around the aircraft was painted to illustrate the shockwaves from the explosion. The pictures on the next page follow the building process of the explosion:

*Cutting holes in the fuselage*

*Placing LED and halogen lamps*

*Testing lamps*

*Making blast waves on the «sea»*

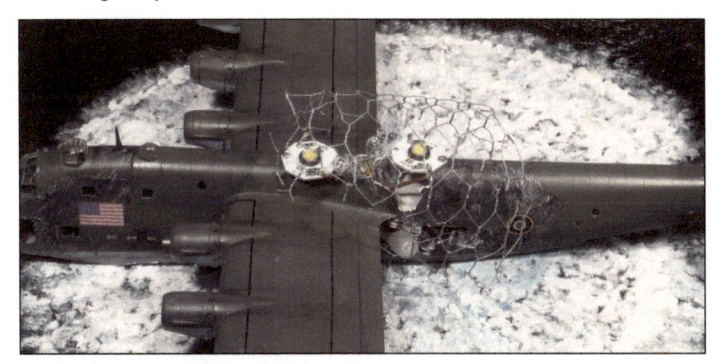

*Building a chicken wire cage*

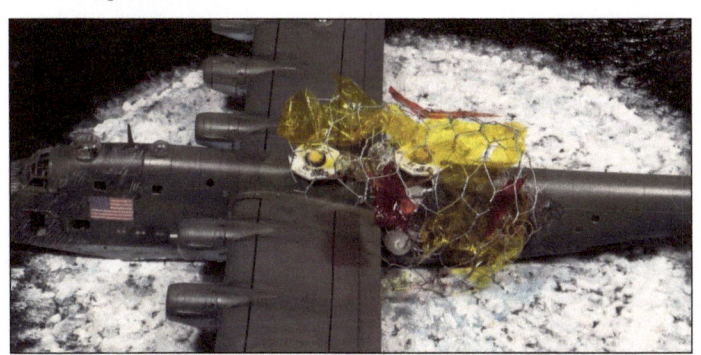

*Adding yellow and red cellophane*

*Adding cotton to the chicken wires*

*Painting the cotton (airbrush)*

53

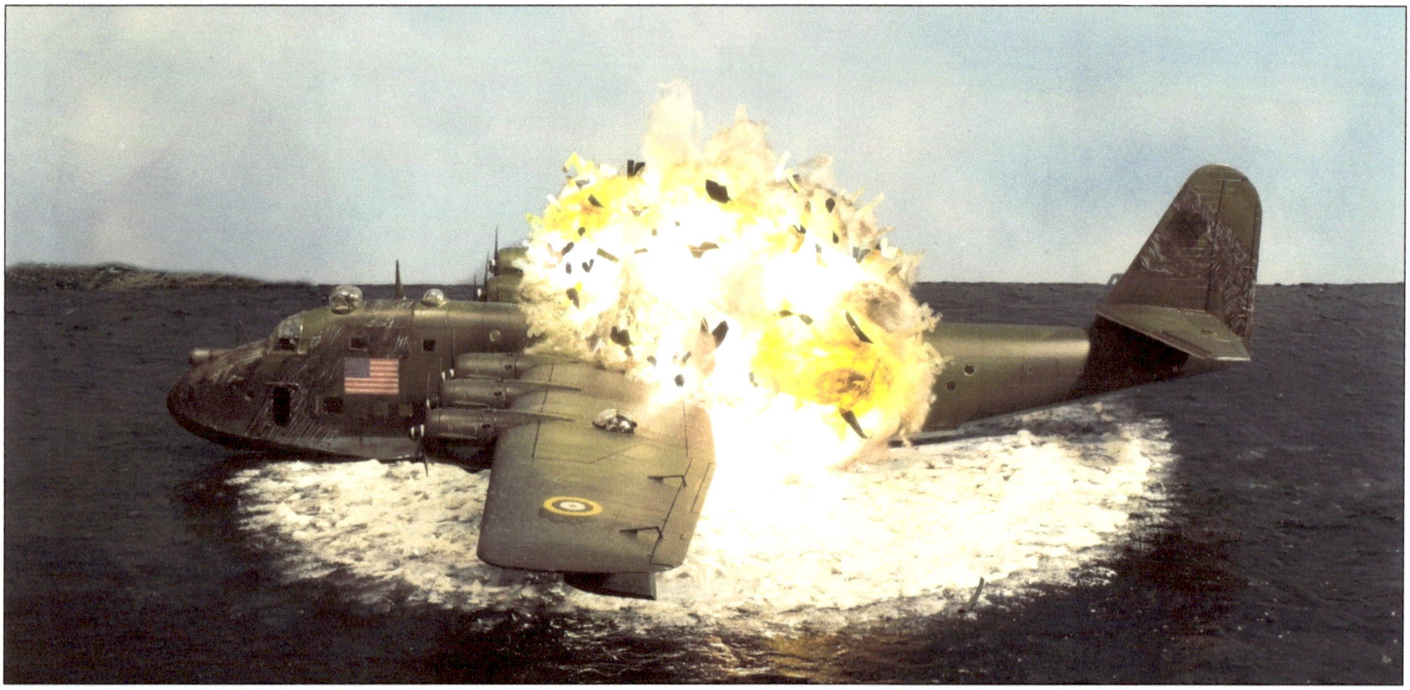

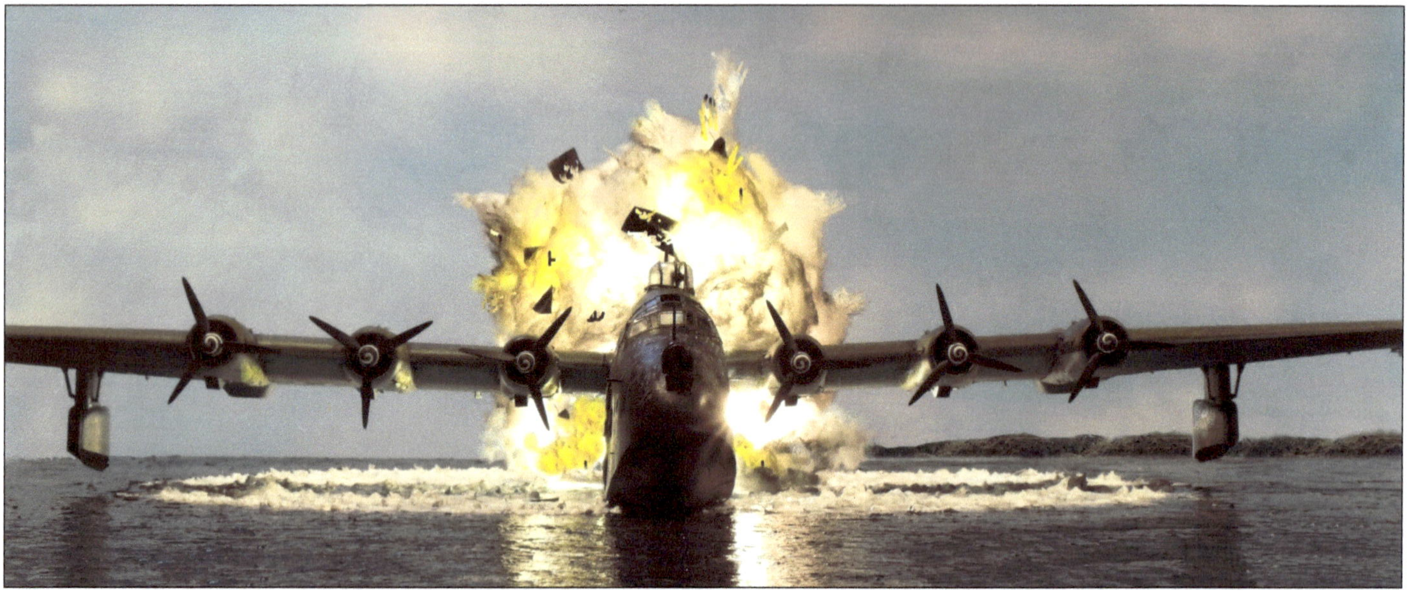

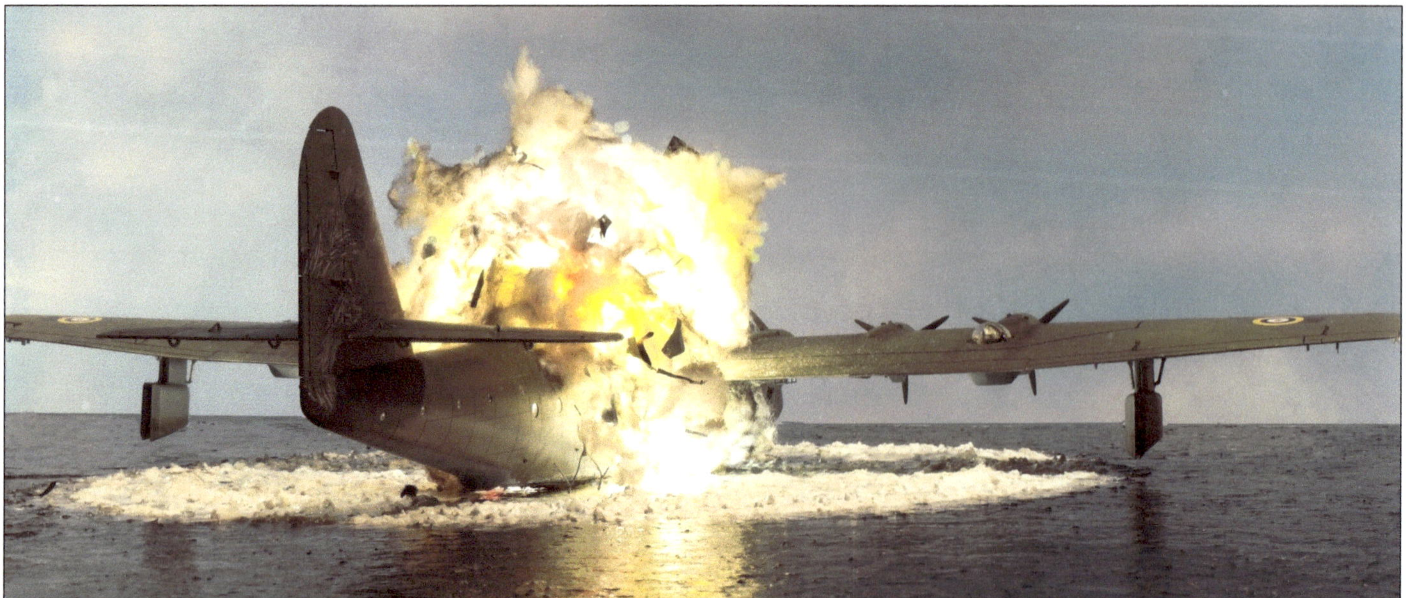

55

**The next two dioramas are not really dioramas in the normal sense; it's more of a storytelling project. Why?**

Because the incidents described in these projects are truly amazing and important. The problem seen from a diorama view is that the scales of the models involved are so different that it would not be practical to make a static diorama that tells the story. So, bear with me, these are not dioramas to be displayed, but I believe that the dioramas, the models and the pictures melt together in a great pictorial story.
I hope this might inspire some of you to try something similar. It's a lot of fun!
**The dioramas are: "The Battle of Midway" and "Taranto"**

# The Battle of Midway
### the story of the Douglas SBD Dauntless

**4th of June 1942: One airplane turned the disastrous tide for the Americans and changed a potentially damaging defeat into the US Navy's proudest victory of World War II**

Six months after Pearl Harbor, this one-day battle reversed the tide of war in the Pacific, this is the story in short:
Almost the entire Japanese fleet participated in the invasion of Midway: Six aircraft carriers, eleven battleships, thirteen cruisers, forty-five destroyers, assorted submarines, transports and minesweepers. The Japanese calculated that when the United States began its counterattack, the Japanese Imperial Fleet would crush them.
Against this enormous fleet, the American forces seem rather tiny: Three aircraft carriers, eight cruisers, fourteen destroyers, and the aircraft stationed on Midway itself. However, the Americans had solved the Japanese fleet codes and knew about their plan and sent their torpedo bombers to attack the Japanese carriers. The initial attack was a disaster. 36 out of 42 bombers were shot down and none of the carriers were hit.
To follow up on their earlier attack on Midway, the Japanese armed their bombers and the Zeros defending the fleet returned to their carriers for rearming and refuelling. At this crucial moment, the American Dauntless dive-bombers appeared over the Japanese fleet. The Japanese defenders failed to notice the SBD dive-bombers flying at high altitude. With their decks crammed with planes about to take off, the Japanese carriers were prime targets.
The first attack took out the flight deck of the flagship 'Akagi' detonating a store of torpedoes, the 'Akagi' was doomed. Other SBDs attacked the 'Kaga'. Here again, fuel was soon ignited and the ship suffered severe damage and sank. More dive-bombers attacked the 'Soryu' with the same deadly impact. The last carrier was the 'Hiryu', which was found and attacked with the same devastating consequences as the other three carriers.
The consequences of the Battle of Midway for the Japanese were huge.
At a stroke, they had lost four vital aircraft carriers - the entire strength of the task force - with 322 aircraft and over five thousand sailors of which many were elite pilots and highly experienced ground crews and mechanics.
American losses included 147 aircraft and more than three hundred seamen.

# The Diorama:

I am going to use my models to tell the story of the SBD dive-bombers. From the take-off from the US carriers to the destruction of the four Japanese Aircraft Carriers. Of course, it is impossible to make a diorama covering all this, so I have to settle for pictures of the Dauntless on deck and in flight and concentrate the actual diorama to the bombing of the Japanese carrier Akagi.
For the Dauntless, I choose the 1:48 scale, for the warships, I used the Akagi and the light cruiser in 1/700. For the Pacific, I had to settle for a plywood board.

# Building the Akagi aircraft carrier and the light cruiser

To make the ships as realistic as possible, I used some cotton to make smoke pouring out of the ship's funnels. The Akagi was hit by three 1000lb bombs, one in the middle of the flight deck and two extremely close to the port side.

I cut a hole in the deck and placed a 12V halogen lamp in the opening. The electrical wires will be hidden under the diorama base. To make the colour of the explosion more realistic, I put some red and yellow cellophane inside the cotton. Besides the actual bomb blast, a lot of aviation fuel ignited on the deck.

# The Pacific

The Pacific base is a plywood plate 71 x 87 cm (28 x 35 in)

It was painted dark blue with the white wakes from the Japanese ships desperate manoeuvring.
I covered the whole "sea" with clear silicon, using a spoon to make the "waves" and "space" for the carrier and the escort ship.

The silicone was good at making bomb and shell impacts in the water. What it was not good at, was to add additional paint to the surface.
Of course, I should have known that acrylic paint on silicone is a no-no.

Then I painted a background and included smoke from a burning Japanese carrier.
I used Akagi both with and without the bomb blast because I photographed the scenario before and after the bomb hit the deck.
The Agagi with the bomb blast made a good background when photographing the SBDs getaway from the burning carrier.

# The Douglas SBD Dauntless dive-bomber

The SBD model I used was made in 1/48 scale.
When SBD operated in the Pacific, the crew often flew with an open cockpit.
So also in this model.
The weathering on aircraft operating from the carriers relates mostly to oil spill from the engines (the radial engines was always leaking oil), some exhaust stains and of course the wear and tear on the paint.
The challenge in this build was the bomb rack, the flaps, the landing gears and the dive brakes.
The reason is I want pictures of this plane on the carrier deck, ready for take-off and pictures of the flight towards the Japanese Navy . I also want pictures of the SBD dive-bombing the carrier Akagi.
That means the landing gear should be both out and in retracted position. The dive brake should be fully employed and fully pulled in. The bomb should be secured to the aircraft and dropped during the dive bombing.
Since none of these parts was movable on this model, I just had to improvise, mostly by glueing the parts lightly so they could easily be removed and glued in different positions.

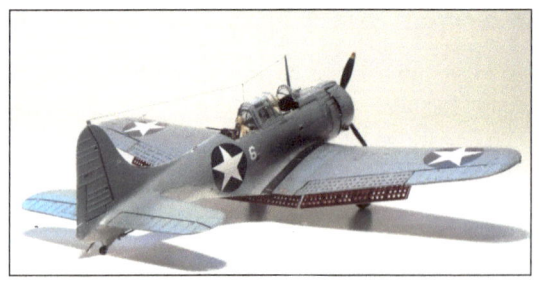

*The model had propeller attached to a plastic rod which serve as propeller shaft when correctly lubricated. I sanded the shaft and lubricated it with dry graphite. With a help of a little wind, the propeller rotated perfectly. In the pictures to the left, I blow at the propeller. This means I can take very realistic pictures of the aircraft in the air or on the carrier deck.*

*SBD Dauntless warming up prior to launch from the carrier deck.
The deck and the background are painted cardboard. The propeller is spinning thanks to a light breeze from my wife's hairdryer.*

The SBDs – nicknamed "Slow But Deadly" - are ready for take-off from the carrier deck

The picture above is made by mixing pictures of the model in three different positions on the deck (#1, #2, #3)
I used the picture of the front aircraft (#3) as the base and pasted the two other pictures (# 2 and 3) on the first one.
The first series of three pictures shows the three different original pictures. The series below shows the sequence in which the original pictures were used.
Of course, you need a photo editing program to do this.

In the picture above, I pasted the SBD model into a b/w picture of a carrier. I let everything be b/w and hoped it would look like and old WW2 picture. Showing the lift-off of an SBD dive-bomber.

To the right:
The diorama with the exploding bomb on Akagi's deck.
The next step will be to paste the American dive-bombers to the diorama background.

*The impacts of cannon fire on the water was made by the same clear silicon as used for the sea surface.*

59

To make the pictures of the SDBs on their way to, and attacking the Japanese Fleet, I needed a suitable background.
I found a picture of an ocean from above and used the photo editing program to airbrush some clouds, the wakes from the Japanese ships and a few AAA-blasts to make the picture as «real» as possible.
To make the picture to the left, different pictures of the model were "cut out" (pasted) and placed in different positions on the new background picture. Placed in different sizes and angles it looks like the SBDs are attacking the Japanese carrier.

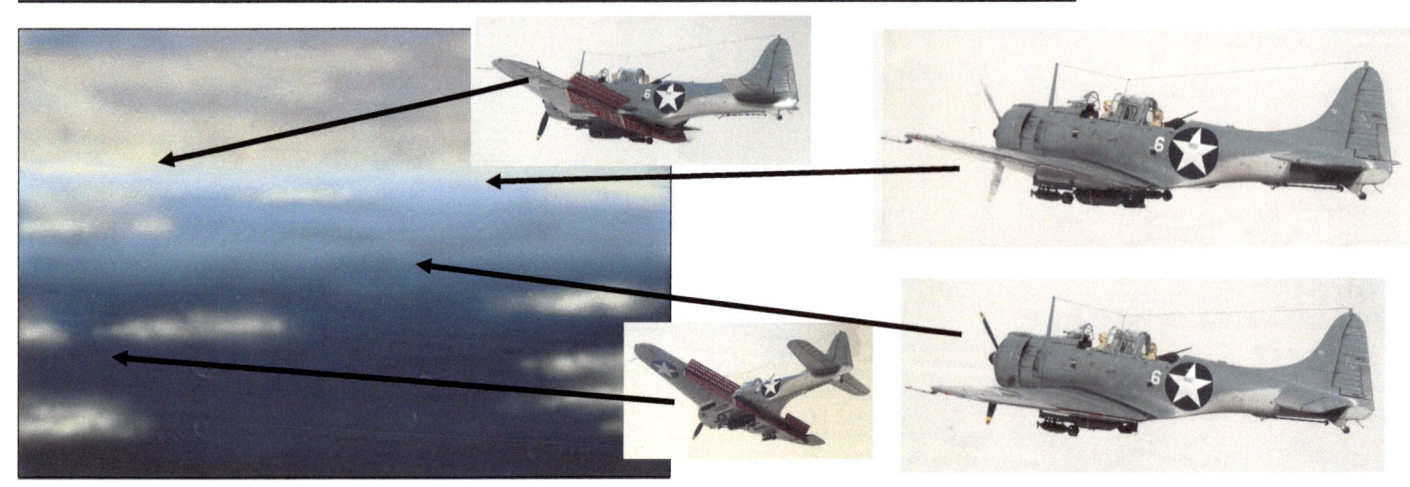

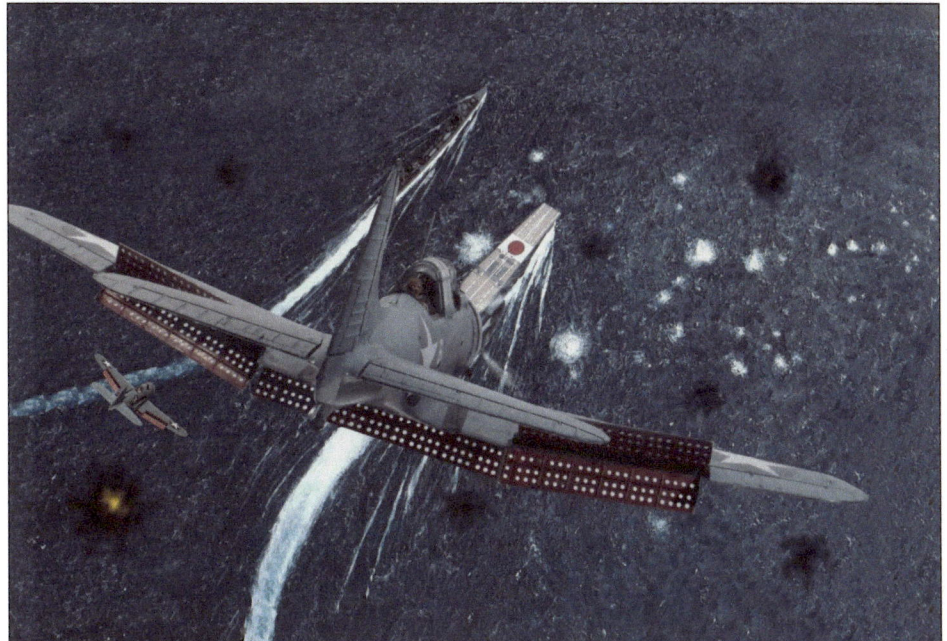

In this picture, I used the same background as on the previous page and pasted a couple of SBDs diving towards the Japanese Carrier with airbrakes fully employed.

Here I used the diorama base as background and pasted a couple of SBD diving on the Agaki carrier.

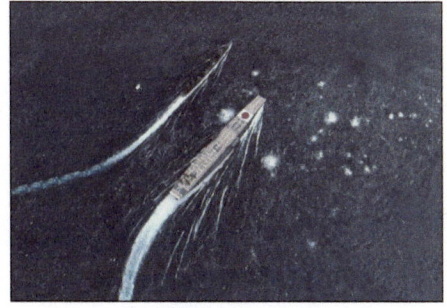

Bomb away!
On this picture, I actually used the picture of the model (no pasting). I only "painted" some smoke and grenade blasts by the help of the photo editing program and tilted the picture a little.
I took a picture of the bomb and pasted it underneath the aircraft.

61

As many times before, I used the Photo Edit Program to paste my models into a new and more exciting background. To the left, you see the two backgrounds used for these two pictures. To the left is diorama background, the one of the carrier is a background I painted especially for this picture.

# The "Stringbags" at war
## The Battle of Taranto (Italy) 11 November 1940
This is the second diorama, which is not an ordinary static diorama,
but more like a story based on models and diorama

Twenty slow moving and outdated Fairley "Swordfish" decimated the world's perhaps largest battle fleet in Taranto harbour on 11 November 1940.
The British holdings in the Mediterranean were under attack. Axis advances were threatening Crete. Malta was under heavy attack, and Hitler had his eye on the key chokepoint at Gibraltar.
The Germans didn't have a large naval presence in the Mediterranean, but the Italians did – far stronger than the British.
The British had to do something with the mighty Italian fleet and decided to use aircraft from the carrier HMS Illustrious.
On the night of November 11, 1940, a strike force of 20 Swordfish was ready for Taranto.

6 battleships, 7 heavy cruisers, 2 light cruisers and 28 destroyers were waiting for them in the Italian harbour. In addition, the Italians had anti-torpedo nets, 22 searchlights, 21 batteries of 102mm (4in) guns, 101 anti-aircrafts guns and 84 heavy and 109 light machine guns sited to cover the whole area of the port.

The old-fashioned slow moving double-deckers, affectionately called the "Stringbag", were to enter this inferno at a speed of less than 120 mph (195km/t) and only 9 m (30 feet) above the sea.
The big battleships were their priority targets.

### Against all odds, the "Stringbags" succeeded!

Only two aircraft were shot down. All the rest of the Swordfish landed safely on HMS Illustrious.
But the Italian warships were not so lucky:
Three battleships were destroyed. Italy's power had been seriously damaged, and its battleship force had been cut in half.

*This is the diorama base (70x90 cm, 28x36 inches) of the Taranto harbour.*
*Most of this project take place here.*
*The LED lamps light up the explosions from the torpedoes.*
*The pictures have been taken in a rather dark room where the main lights are the explosions. Of course, that means a long exposure (15-20 seconds) and definitely the needs for a tripod.*

# Building the diorama

This will be more challenging than normal because the attack on Taranto happened at night. Everything was pitch black except for the flairs dropped from the Swordfishes, the fires and the exploding shells from hundreds of cannons on shore, on floats and on the ships. Besides, we are talking about a huge harbour with several really big battleships – and a few small double-deckers trying to sink all the battleships...

## The ships

I decided to use two battleships and two destroyers in the diorama (scale 1/700).
I had no model kits of the Italian battleships, so I had to use other models. One of the battleships had an explosion after a torpedo hit; the other had a huge fire.
I made holes in the ship's hull, big enough to insert a small 12V halogen lamp. Then I drilled a hole in the base for the electrical cables and screwed the ships in place with the lamps inside.
For the smoke, I used cotton which I sprayed with black colour. The smoke from the fire was fixed to a wire.

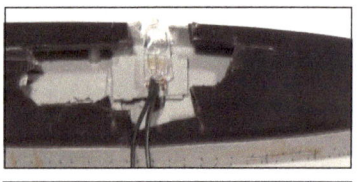

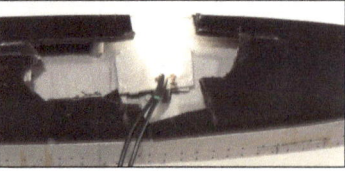

*The explosion and fire in the two battleships were created by small 12V halogen lamps placed inside the hulls. The wires go through a hole in the base.*

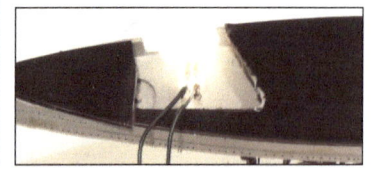

## The base

The base was a plywood plate (70x90cm, 28x36inch) which was painted black. I placed the two battleships on the base and painted the explosion sites besides the hulls.
I also painted quite a few shell impacts on the water and covered the whole area with Realistic Water (Woodland) to give it a "wet" surface. The grenade impact in the water was made by Water Effects by Woodland

## The background

I painted the background on a cardboard plate, mostly very dark, but with some searchlights and a lot of exploding shells.
In front of the backdrop, I needed the harbour, which I made of cardboard and styrofoam.
Behind the docks, was quite a few cannon batteries. I used some leftover Christmas lights to give the illusion of cannon flares.

## The camouflage colours on the Swordfish

There seems to be some confusion about the colours on the Stringbags which took part in the Taranto attack. The normal colours were Extra Dark Sea Grey / Dark Slate Grey (a greenish colour) on upper surfaces; Sky Grey undersides and lower fuselage.

However, the torpedo planes in the 815 squadron were painted black on the lower wings and lower fuselage in order to blend in as much as possible.

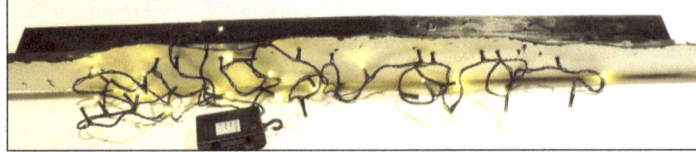

*In the harbour background, I used some Xmas decoration lamps for cannon flares. The harbour was made of styrofoam*

# The Stringbag

The Swordfish I built was in scale 1/48.

The kit was from Tamiya and comes with both torpedo and the extra fuel tank, which was needed for the long flight from the carrier to Taranto and back again.

The only place to have this tank on a Swordfish was in the observer's seat (between the pilot and the gunner) – which of course made the observers/gunners duties a lot more difficult.

The Swordfish was an old construction (first flight was April 1934). It was built with a metal airframe covered in fabric.

I used PE (Photo Etch) for the rigging. There are many different ways to do the rigging and there have been some discussions on how to do it. I did it the following way, which worked very well:

I glued the two wing pair together with the main struts and then fixed all the wires at just one end, leaving the other end to be glued later.

Then I glued the mid-section and the two wing pair together at the same time, and last, when all elements had dried, I fixed the loose ends of the supporting wires.

I needed the propeller to rotate when photographing the aircraft in the air.

This was achieved by lubricating the "propeller shaft" with dry graphite so it would rotate by the slightest wind.

Using my wife's hairdryer did the trick nicely.

*Belov; The Stringbags ready for take-off. This picture was made by pasting two pictures of the model behind the front aircraft. The propellers are really spinning.*

65

All the pictures on these two pages have the model pasted on new backgrounds.
The two pics of the aircraft flying off from the carrier has been pasted on paintings. All the others have been pasted on the diorama background.

These pictures are telling the fantastic story of the Stringbags in action against overwhelming forces. Three battleships were sunk and 18 of 20 Swordfish got back to the carrier safely.

Without the help of a photo editing program, these pictures had not been possible.

# Stuka Pilot Hans-Ulrich Rudel, the best combat pilot

Hans-Ulrich Rudel flew a slow dive-bombing Junkers Ju87.
A plane that normally either had to have escorts to avoid being shot down by enemy fighters or only operates safely in areas with own air supremacy.

It should not be possible to become Germany's most decorated soldier in WWII in the cockpit of a Stuka, but Rudel became a living legend for the German soldiers on the Eastern Front.

He received his baptism of fire as Stuka pilot during the German invasion of the Soviet Union in 1941. When the war ended, Rudel had conducted 2519 raids against the Red Army, and he obtained results which seem completely absurd.

In attacks at low altitude, often with fierce anti-aircraft fire against him, he flew the slow and cumbersome Ju87G "Kanonenvogel" against huge Russian armoured forces.

He destroyed at least 519 Russian tanks. He sunk the battleship "Marat", a destroyer and a cruiser (at Kronstadt outside Stalingrad). He sunk at least 70 landing craft (in the Black Sea by the Crimean Peninsula). He bombed and shot to pieces between 800 and 1,000 vehicles and at least 150 artillery pieces.

*Hans-Ulrich Rudel survived the war and died in Germany in 1982*

## The Diorama

In the diorama, Hans-Ulrich Rudel in his Stuka just has blown up a Russian tank. He flies so low that he is flying through the explosion and touches the top of a nearby tree. This is not an entirely unknown manoeuvre of a "Kanonenvogel" on the Eastern Front.

These machines had to fly low. Each of the two aircraft cannons holds only six grenades and every shot had to count. Rudel managed once to destroy six Russian tanks in one raid. It was not unusual that he flew ten or fifteen raids per day. His record was 17 destroyed Russian tanks in a day.

Sometimes the Stukas landed with scorched fuselages with a lot of splinters after flying through exploding tanks.

The first I did was to make a sketch of how I thought the diorama should be. As you can see, there are three main elements in this diorama:

The Base
The Aircraft
The Tank and the Soldiers

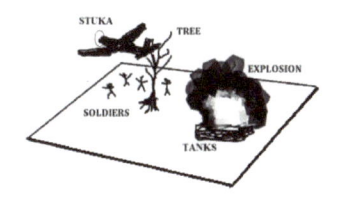

# The Base

A plate from an old kitchen drawer (40 x 50cm) will do nicely. A little joint compound helps form the landscape.
A couple of brass tubes drilled down and glued to the baseplate are starting points for the trees. Tank tracks in the wet filler are made (always difficult to make these tracks later) An electric motor in the Stuka is mounted so the propeller can spin. I thought first to put the electrical cables through the brass tube, but the rod that holds the plane is going in the tube, so I had to place the wires up along the trunk. The wires go through the bottom of the base.
The next task is to make the brass tubes become trees. The inside of an ordinary lamp cord is ideal for making a tree. By twisting the thin brass wires and split them up into smaller "branches" can I make the tree exactly the way I want it. The thin wires are fastened with CA glue when they are laid on the stem. The brass tubes are bent slightly to make the trees more realistic.
Finally, I use Elmer's Clear Glue, to which I added sawdust, on the tree trunks. In this way, the trunks will be roughly like a real tree with bark. Then, the trees need to be painted. The best way to add colour to all the little wires that make up the branches is to use an airbrush.
The ground is part sand, soil and mud, especially where the tanks have run. The acrylic colour is painted directly on the filler. In addition, I sprinkled a little sand to create a bit more "life" to the ground.
I used artificial grass from Woodland Scenics to make grass and bushes around the trees.
This is a battlefield, so I made a couple of craters after grenades or bombs, and place some burnt and bent parts around to illustrate exploded vehicles. For longer grass, I cut some of the bristles from a paintbrush and glued the "straws" on the ground.

# The Aircraft

To make the diorama as realistic as possible I placed an electric motor in the Stuka so the propeller can run. I planned to attach the Stuka to the treetop so it looks like it flies very low. The diorama is in 1:48 scale.
The electric motor (from Airfix) was fitted in the nose. It required some changes in the kit to adapt the engine, but finally, it's glued on with CA-glue.
To attach the plane to the tree, I used a brass rod that fits into the brass tube that was used as a tree. Thus, I can stick the plane into the top of the tree. The brass rod is glued firmly to the inside of the plane.
The wires from the electric motor are moved backwards and will become part of the tree.

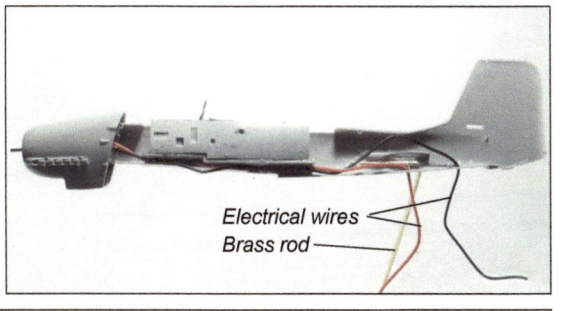

69

# The Tank

I choose a KV-1 which was a heavy 44 tons Russian tank with a crew of 4-5. The scale is the same as the aircraft: 1/48

In the diorama, the tank is hit from behind in the engine compartment. The ammunition explodes after being hit by the Stuka 37 mm cannons and the tower is thrown away.

The inner hull of the model is made of metal, which is good because I want to place a 3W 220VLED light inside the tank. This will be the explosion light. Lights always emit heat, and it's very important to plan for this when making an explosion.

The LED lamp is connected directly to the 220V mains and even if the LED light is not particularly hot, the circuits on the LED board produces heat. I, therefore, drilled a series of holes in the bottom of the tank's metal case to obtain a better cooling.

The tower is blown away, and that means the hot air can escape more easily. However, it is important that the LED light is not on for too long.

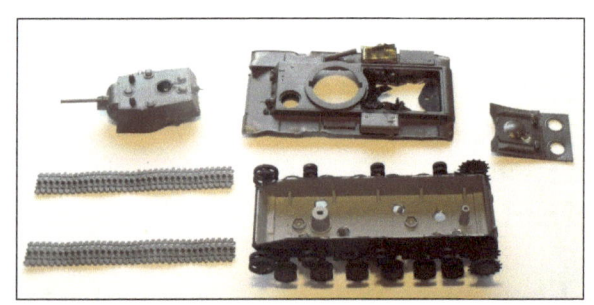

# The Explosion

To build the explosion, I made a skeleton of metal mesh and then drill holes in the tank so I can fasten the wires to the tank. I then put cotton to the metal mesh and made sure there was a large cavity as possible inside the "explosion" to make better cooling. Then the cotton was painted (by airbrush). First yellow, then a little red and finally a dash of black.

The lower tank frame was screwed into the diorama board. The upper part of the tank is loose so it can easily be removed if I have to re-arrange something with the LED light, or if it gets too hot.

Then, last, the tank tower was glued to the metal cage.

# The Power Supply

I have installed two power switches, one for the Stuka and one for the explosion.
The current to the electric motor is 1.5V from a couple AA batteries. The LED is connected to 220V.
I've put a dimmer on LED light so I can reduce the brightness (and heat) if desired.

*Underside of the base* — *The power switches*

# Stuka in the treetop

It was easy to place the Stuka at the top of the tree.
The brass rod from the aircraft went nicely into the brass tube in the tree and a little glue sealed everything in place.
The wires from the engine were connected to the wires coming out of the tree and everything was twisted like branches.
A few leaves were added to make it all look a part of the tree.
I have given the Stuka some dents and scratches after collisions with trees.
It is important to remember that the Stuka was a large and robust machine that could take a lot of beating without hitting the ground. It was almost 11m (36 feet) long, had a 1.300hk engine and weighed 17 tons.

I used some 1/48 Russian soldiers in the diorama to give it some life.
Of course, the soldiers use all their weapons against the Stuka when it passes over.

# The Background

For the diorama to be as realistic and natural as possible it needed a background and I cut a cardboard plate and painted a war scenario that I think fits the diorama.

The battle took place somewhere in the flat landscape of the Eastern Front in fall of 1944. Burning tanks, aircraft, AAA and explosions everywhere.

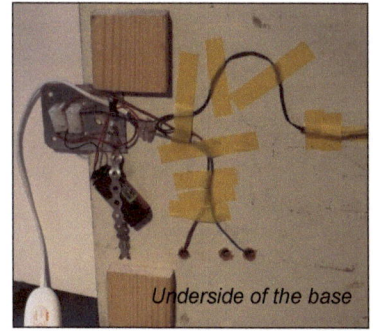

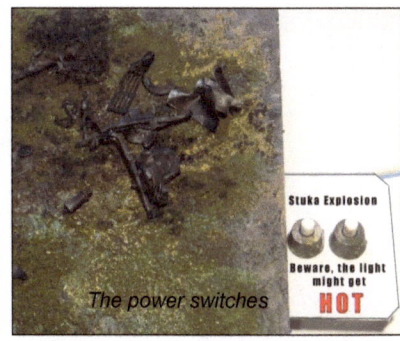

# The Kanonenvogel Diorama

73

# Kurt Knispel, the greatest tank ace of all time

Kurt Knispel destroyed more enemy tanks - Soviet, British and American - than anyone else in history. How many? Nobody knows exactly, but probably around 200.

Allied tanks were being blown away by Knispel and his Tiger tank. He fought in virtually every type of German tank as loader, gunner and commander. He was awarded the Iron Cross, First Class, after destroying his fiftieth enemy tank and the Tank Assault Badge in Gold after more than 100 tank battles. At the famous Panzer Battle at Kursk July 1943, he destroyed twenty-seven T-34 tanks in 12 days.

Later, as commander of a Tiger II, he destroyed another 42 enemy tanks.

Knispel had a very slow promotion which attributed to several conflicts with higher Nazi officers. His behaviour was not up to the Nazi-standard and he cared far more for his mates than for the Nazi system: Long hair, goatee beard, unwillingness to obey orders he disagreed with was one thing, refusing to take part in attacks on civilians was another.

On one occasion, he even attacked an officer when he saw him mistreating a Soviet POW. Most soldiers would have been in a lot of trouble for this, perhaps even executed, but not Knispel. It tells a lot of Knispel's standing, not only within his Panzer Abteilung but in the whole German Panzer Force.

He fought in every major battle at the eastern front from 1941 until the end in 1945, except for a period in spring 1944, when he was transferred to the western front and given command of a new Tiger II, the most fearsome tank in any army. He participated in fighting the Allied after the invasion in Normandy and he fought in the defence of Caen.

After the Caen, Knispel returned to the East and fought in the Budapest area, where some of the hardest fightings of the last year of the war took place. One week before the war ended, he was fatally wounded during battles against huge numbers of T-34 in Southern Czechoslovakia after Budapest and Vienna had fallen.

# The Russian T-34/85

There will be three Russian Tanks in the diorama (Scale 1/48). The Tiger with Kurt Knispel as gunner opens fire on the Russian tanks and in about 20 seconds (it takes ten seconds to reload the Tigers 88mm), all three T-34s are ready for the scrap yard. The first one is hit in the engine department and burst immediately into flames. The second is hit just below the tower and when the T-34s shells explode, the tank tower is ripped off the tank.

The third tank is still intact in the diorama, but with Knispels precise targeting, it will be an easy kill in a few moments.

To make the explosions and fire, I used LED lamps (220V). The advantages with these LED lamps are that they emit very little heat and can easily be used in the confined spaces in a plastic model.

The first hit in the engine requires some black smoke and I used the "normal" procedure with the chicken wire cage, some coloured cellophane and cotton fitted to the wire cage and painted with airbrush.

It's important to have the cotton as thin as possible. Too dense cotton will usually not look like smoke.

*Above: Tank # 1 has not yet been hit by the Tiger and is still intact. The commander in the tower has just discovered the German tank.*

*Above: Tank # 2 has been hit below the tower and is blowing up. A LED light inside the tank gives the explosion light. The tower is being ripped off.*

*Left and below: Tank # 3 was the first tank to be hit by the Tiger. It was hit in the engine department and burst into fire. A chicken wire cage, cellophane, cotton and airbrush colour makes the explosion and fire. The electrical wires will be led through the base and hidden from sight.*

# The Tiger tank

The model is a 1:35, compared to the Soviet tanks 1:48. This has to do with the perspective; the Soviet tanks are at a distance and needed to be smaller.

I tried to build the Tiger as a real battle tank, with scars and wounds after several engagements with overwhelming enemy forces.

The Tiger was a real tough beast and could take a lot of punishment and still fight on. I, therefore, rip off a side shirt and gave it a lot of grenade hits.

The tank was part of sPzAbt. 503, 1st Company, 1st Platoon and tanks nr.2 with Kurt Knispel as Richtschütze (Gunner).

The Richtschütze was responsible for the all hits his tank made.

Under an engagement, he had to stay on his post under the open hatch on the right side of the tower. On the left side is the tank commander.

The tiger had a crew of five; Tank Commander, gunner, loader, driver and radio operator.

The diorama freezes the moment the Tiger fires its second shot and hits the T-34 just below the tower.

Therefore, I need gun smoke from the Tiger's gun barrel as well as the impact in the T-34.

The gun smoke is just cotton, sprayed with hairspray to stiffen and then slightly coloured with the airbrush.

The hairspray makes the cotton so stiff that it without problem can be added directly to the cannon muzzle.

I first painted the Tank Commander in a camouflage uniform, but I soon realized that the Heer's Panzer Waffen always wore the black Panzer Uniform. I, therefore, repainted the uniform (on the pictures, you might see both the first and the second uniform).

I also placed a canvas on the turret bin but discovered that this was blocking the view from the cupola, so I removed it before placing the tank in the diorama.

## The Soldiers

I used 1:35 German soldiers (Military Miniatures from Tamiya) and 1:48 Russian soldiers (Russian Infantry from Tamiya) to make the diorama more authentic.

## The Burned-out Houses

The Russian tanks are next to a burned-out village. The houses were made by glueing wooden sticks to a simple fundament made of cardboard (nothing fancy).

Then it was painted with acrylic colours.

All the rubbish around is just bits and pieces of cardboard and wooden sticks. All very easy and very cheap, but it looked good.

# The Base

Sometimes you do not fully understand the consequences of what you have started. The Base is a good example. I was planning "A medium size diorama" and started out with a 1:35 Tiger and several 1:48 T-34s which have to be at some distance from each other. It soon occurs to me that this would be a diorama, much bigger than I had planned! I decided to do the base in two parts: One with the Tiger and one with the T-34s. When I put the two parts together, the dimension was 70x120cm (28" x 48"). The good thing was that the diorama took less space when stored and it was easier to handle.

The first I did was to make terrain with Styrofoam which I later covered with papier Mache and painted the whole surface with acrylic colours. When finished, it's time for the props (burned out houses, tanks and soldiers). Then I covered the fields with artificial grass and put up some trees and bushes for good measures. The last thing I did was to paint a background on a cardboard.

77

# The Diorama

The trees behind the burnt houses are branches from a hedge in my back yard.
The bushes are bought from a hobby shop. All the big trees in the background are part of the painted backdrop.
The "bomb"-craters are carved out of the paper Mache ground and painted.

The grass on the field was made of electrostatic grass. The area is first painted with acrylic and then covered with clear liquid glue. The grass fibres are electrostatically charged (by a 9v battery) and when the "grass" are sprinkled over the area, the fibres land in a vertical position in the glue on the ground—and stays that way. The grass comes in many colours and lengths and is very easy to apply. For longer grass (or reeds) I use to cut fibres off an old paintbrush and glue on the ground.

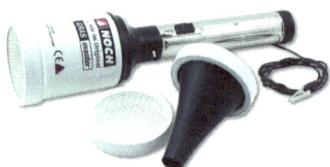

Kurt Knipsel Diorama

81

## Kurt Knispel - King Tiger Commander

In this diorama, I have placed the greatest tank ace of all time, Kurt Knispel, as commander in the turret of his King Tiger, some place in France in 1944.
During his career, he officially destroyed 168 enemy tanks (126 as a Gunner and 42 as a Commander), but his actual score was much larger, probably as high as around two hundred.
He was a soldier in a war, led by one of the worst regimes ever, but he was not a Nazi, far from it. He was as anti-Nazi as it was possible to be, without being executed or transferred to a penal battalion. His behaviour was far from the Nazi standard and he cared far more for his mates than for the Nazi system: Long hair, goatee- beard (he frequently told his commander he had no time for shaving), unwillingness to obey orders he disagreed with was one thing, refusing to take part in attacks on civilians was another.
He even attacked a soldier when he saw him mistreating a Soviet POW, punched him in the face and broke his gun! That was the kind of guy he was!
No wonder he was never promoted beyond Feldwebel (Sergeant).

He remained an anonymous soldier in the German Heer until his tragic death only a week before the end of World War 2.

### The figure of Kurt Knispel

I wanted him to be seen in the commander hatch. No Kurt Knispel figure was available, so I had to make one myself.
By taking an ordinary figure and using normal filler I tried to sculpture a figure that could pass for Knispel.
He was famous (at least after the war) for his un-military rebel hair and goatee. Of course, he was ordered to shave from time to time and it is no proof that he had the goatee as a Tank Commander.
But the jagged appearance is the "picture" most of us have of him, and that's what I attempted to create.

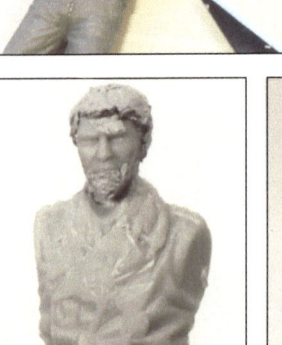

# The Base

The base was 35 x 45 cm (14" x 18") plywood on which I glued some Polyurethane to make the terrain I wanted.
Then I covered the whole with paper Mache, added some stones in what I hoped should be a small creek and painted everything with acrylic paint.
The next step was to put on some grass, bushes, a log and last, but not least: some water in the creek (Woodland Realistic Water)
The grass was mostly electrostatic grass (see page 80).
The log was from a tree in my back yard and the bushes some cheap stuff I bought from a hobby shop.

# The King Tiger

The tank was in scale 1.35

The track and the lower hull were painted in the same muddy, dirty colours and the rim of the tracks were brushed with steel colour.

If you look at pictures of the King Tiger at the battlefield, you will see that some had removed the side fenders entirely, others have part of them ripped off, while some had all the fenders intact.

Knispel's tank was in the front of the battle almost all the time and had a lot of damages.
One time he counted 28 hits by enemy grenades after a battle.
I, therefore, made several grenade damages on the hull and the turret and ripped off some of the side fenders for good measures. To make the bent fenders more believable, I placed thin metal sheets instead of the "thick" plastic parts.

I decided to paint the tank in a three-colour scheme; Dark Yellow, Dark Green and Red/Brown with mottling of the same colours.
The weathering is rather extensive, because this is a fighting vehicle in a muddy and dirty battlefield.

The background is a painted cardboard. Painted with airbrush (the sky) and hand brush (the woods).

All the German soldiers and the tank crew are from different kits and are all in 1/35 scale

The grass is electrostatic grass.

This is the second Kurt Knispel diorama in this book. The first is on pages 74-81 and show his tank destroying tree Soviet tanks.

# The Katyusha

The BM-series "Katyusha" was the first multiple mobile rocket launcher in World War II. The launcher was usually mounted on ordinary trucks. This mobility gave the Katyusha the advantage of delivering a large blow to the enemy, and then quickly move before being located and attacked with counter-battery fire.

German troops nicknamed the Katyusha as Stalin's Organ (German: Stalinorgel) because of the terrible howling sound when the rockets were launched. The weapon was less accurate than conventional artillery guns, but was extremely effective in saturation bombardment, and was particularly feared by German soldiers.

Katyusha batteries were often used in large numbers to create a shock effect on enemy forces. By the end of the war, 10,000 Katyusha launchers were produced along with 12 million rockets

## The Katyusha Nickname

The original BM-13 launchers were manufactured at a plant known as the Voronezh Komintern and accordingly bore a large "K" stamp on the side. Troops joked that the letter stood for Katyusha – the name of a popular 1938 folk ballad about a woman who is separated from her lover.
The name soon caught on.

## The Katyusha trucks

The Katyusha never operated as a single unit. They were often employed in great numbers, often several batteries at a time.
A battery of BM-13 launchers included four firing vehicles; two reload trucks and two technical support trucks. Each firing vehicle had a crew of six.
The Katyusha vehicles had no markings; it was just one of thousands of USSR weapons and painted in a grey/green colour.

# The Katyusha Rockets

I wanted the Katyusha to launch the rockets in the diorama and used the following method:

The launching rockets were glued to a 1mm (3/64in) thick metal rod. The rod lengths differed from rocket to rocket. School glue was used to fix cotton to the rods to illustrate the smoke.

A small 10w 12V halogen lamp was fixed to each rod just behind the rocket. The lamp and the wires were fixed to the rod by a very thin metal wire taken from an electrical cable. Then the cotton was sprayed with grey/black colour and let to dry.

To complete the launching rockets, I adjusted the cotton (removed some and covered the wires with some) and painted the part of the wires that was still visible.

At last, the wires were pulled down through the rails and the launching construction and ended underneath the truck. These wires would, of course, be concealed when the trucks were placed on the diorama base.

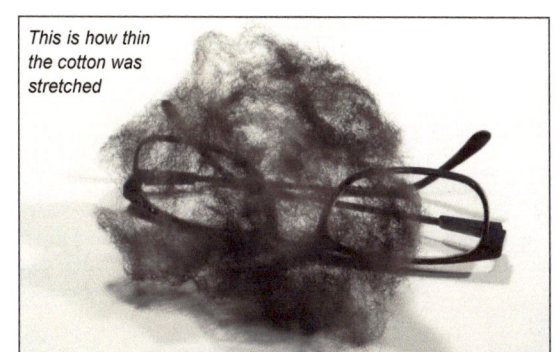

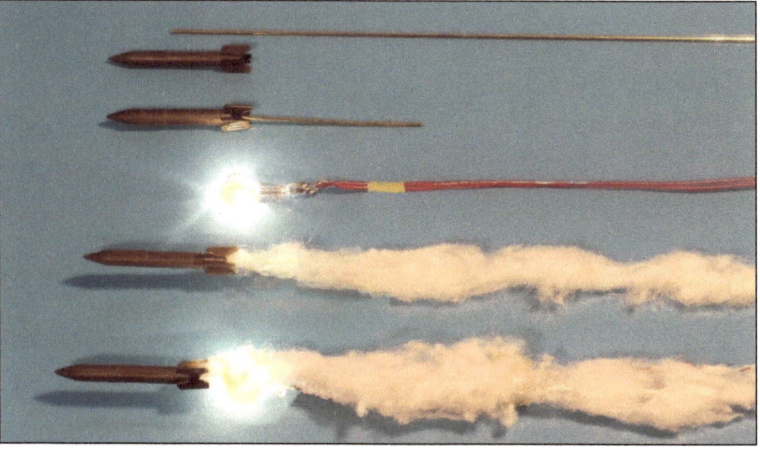

*This is how thin the cotton was stretched*

# The smoke

The rockets produced a lot of smokes when launched and the trucks were covered in smoke. It is always important to have smoke looks as natural as possible. In this case, I used a very fine cotton taken from a medical compress and stretched it as thin as possible. Then I used the airbrush and made it grey/black. Now I could form it any way I wanted, I could make it more compact by pressing it together and thinner by stretching it.

*The result was like this.*
*The electrical wires will be led through a hole in the diorama base and thus be invisible for the viewer when the diorama is finished.*

87

# The base and background

I used a wooden base of 60 x 60 cm (24 x 24 inches).

The terrain was sculpted by paper Mache and the grass is electrostatic grass.

The background is just a painted cardboard.

The figures are part of the Katyusha kits (1/35)

## Please note:

I made two Katyusha launchers. In some of the pictures, you will see three or four launchers (four launchers = a platoon).

I made those pictures by pasting the two vehicles twice (with the use of photo editing)

*The Katyushas on their way to the launching site*

A battery of four BM-13 launchers could fire a salvo of 16x4 rockets in 7–10 seconds, delivering 4.35 tons of high explosives over a 400.000 sq.meters (4,300,000 sq ft) impact zone, roughly equivalent to 72 artillery batteries.

Katyusha batteries were often massed in large numbers to create a shock effect on the enemy forces.

The weapon's disadvantage was the long time it took to reload a launcher, in contrast to conventional guns which could sustain a continuous low rate of fire.

89

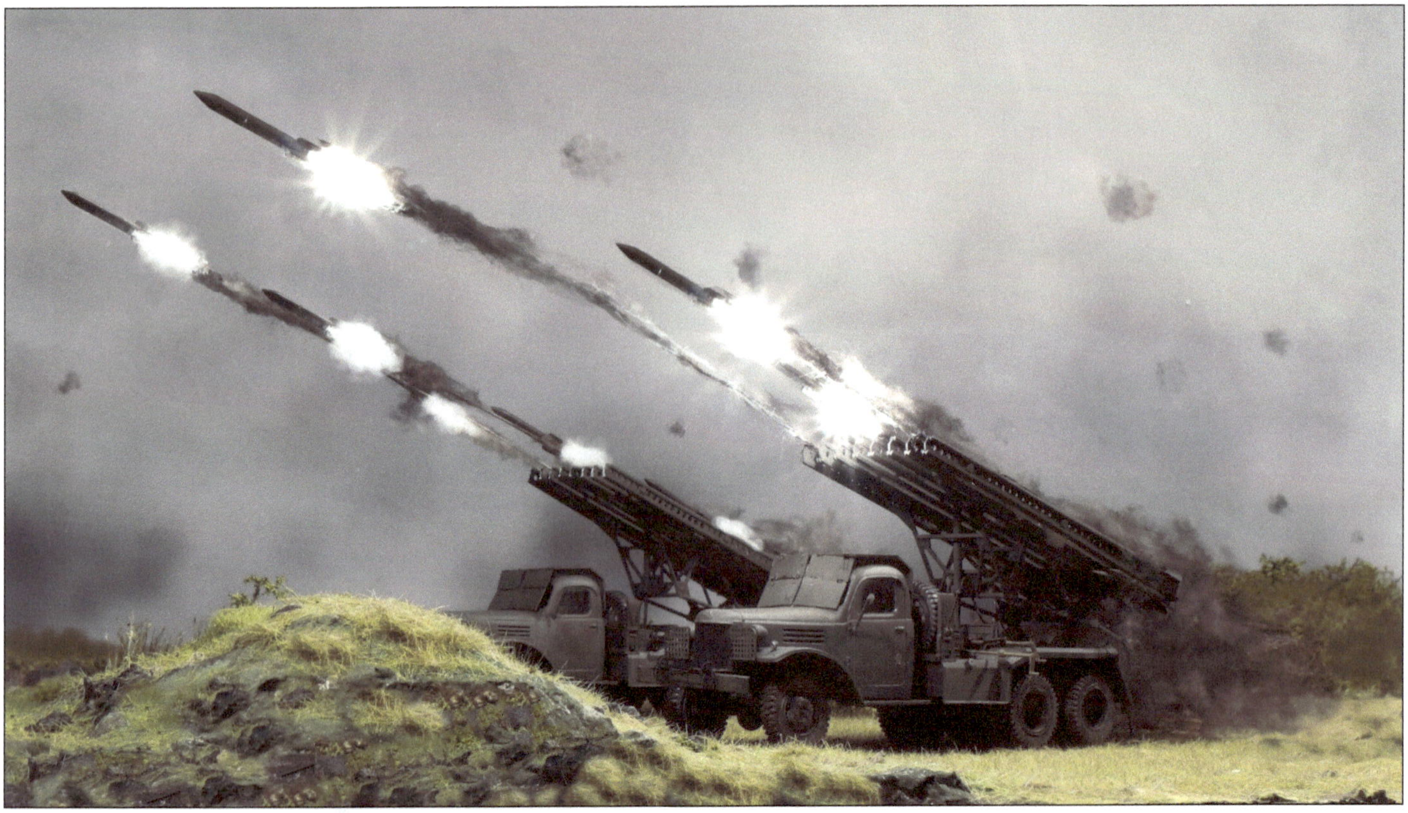

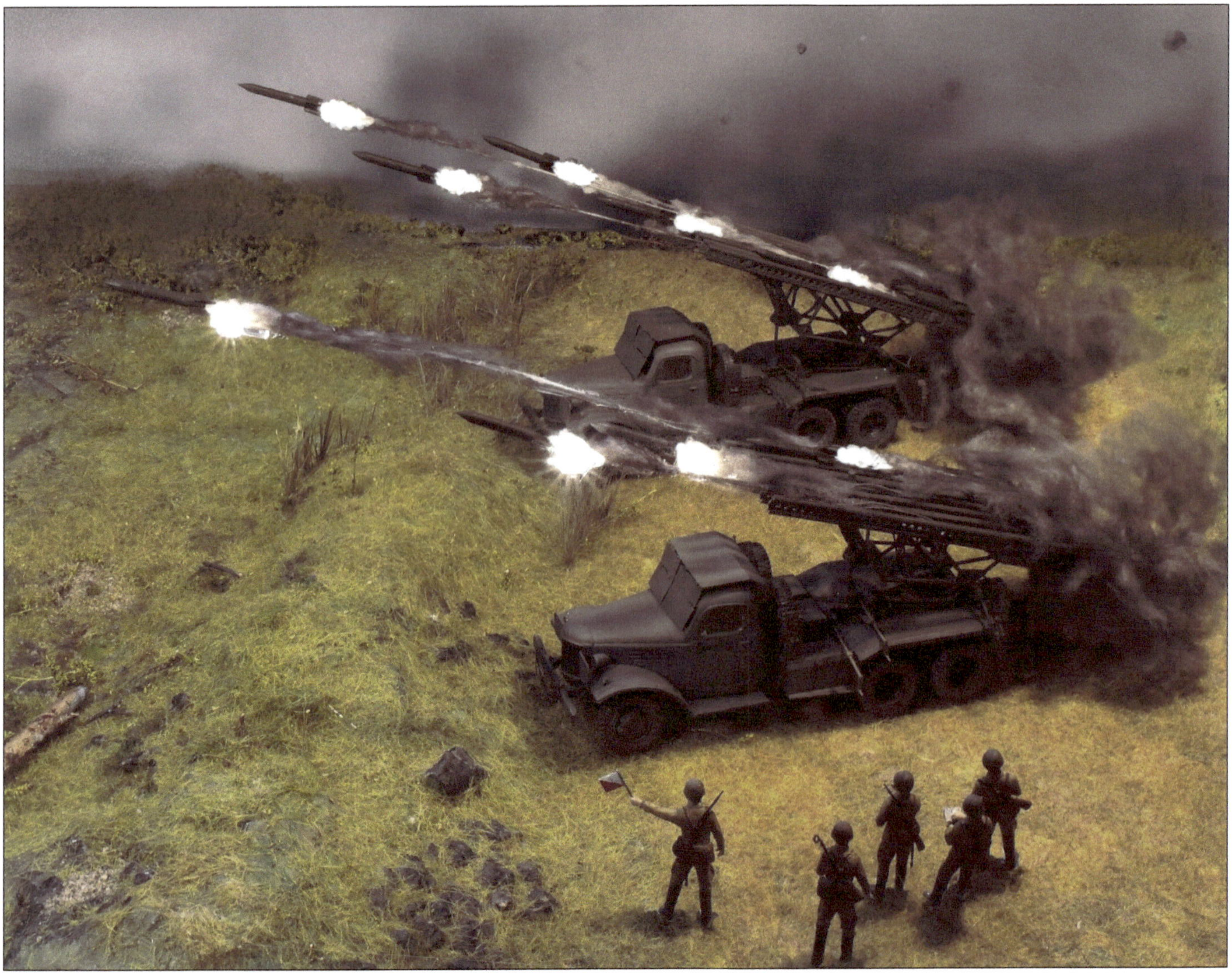

91

# Launching the SA-2 "Guideline" Missile

This SA-2 launch diorama was built in connection with a U-2 project where I made a model of the high-altitude Lockheed U-2 aircraft and the SA-2 missile. What's of interest in this connection is the launching of the missile.

The U2 (not the music band) was an American spy plane that was shot down over the Soviet Union on 1st May 1960 and created a major crisis between the USA and the Soviet Union.

The missile the Soviet used to bring down the U-2 was an SA-2 (NATO codename: Guideline). It was a simple two-stage missile design with three sets of four cruciform fins.

*The 1/35 model of the SA-2 standing on the launch pad*

*The two pictures of the aircraft in the air are pictures of the U-2 model (1/48) which are pasted on different backgrounds.*

# Building the SA-2 launch

The SA-2 with Launchpad was in scale 1:35.

To make the launching picture as realistic as possible, I added some light into the booster to create light from the rocket engine.

For this, I used a clear acrylic tube and inserted a 12V halogen lamp into one end. The tube was then fixed to the rocket booster and the launch rail.

The very thin wires were hidden in the smoke from the rocket.
The smoke from the launch was so widespread that I had to use a chicken wire cage to form the smoke.

After the cotton was fixed to the cage, it was sprayed with hairspray to stiffen.
Finally, I sprayed a little colour on the smoke. Not much, because the smoke was mostly white.

The missile is painted light grey and the colour on the launcher is green. The SA-2 launcher was placed on a green carpet which was painted a little dirty, decorated with some sand and pebbles.
Artificial bushes and trees and a couple of buildings made of cardboard were added to the base.

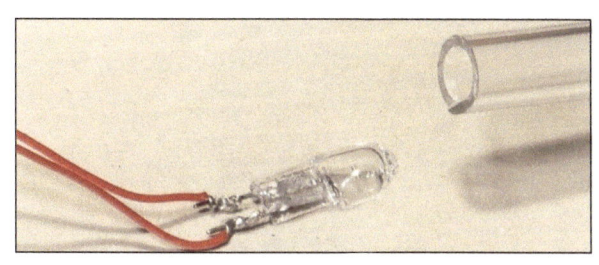

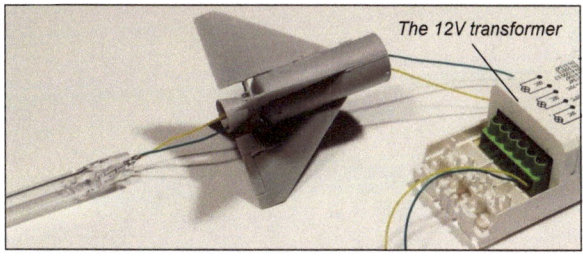

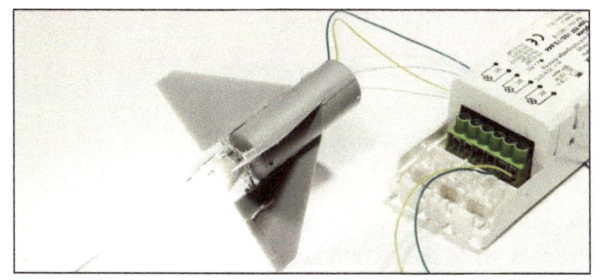

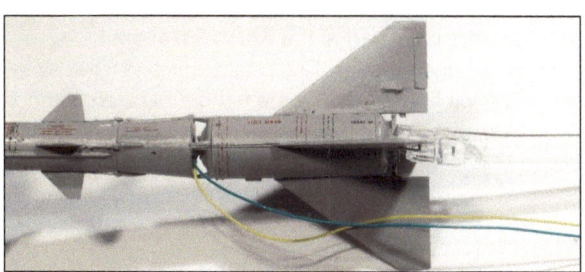

*The 12V transformer*

*The missiles were launched from mobile platforms. Once launched, its main booster burns for 4-5 seconds before the primary motor ignites and burns for another 22 seconds. The warhead of the missile is filled with 130 kg (287 pounds) high explosive*

I used a small 12V halogen lamp which was inserted in the acrylic tube.

The 12V lamp was connected to a (220V) transformer. The lamp did not produce much heat but gave a lot of light.

How long it would be before the heat damaged the tube or the model, I do not know, simply because it was not on more than 3-4 minutes at a time.

And at that time, the heat was not a problem at all.

**But, beware: It is always a danger of over-heating, so never let the lights on unattended!**

The acrylic tube with the 12V lamp was glued to the launcher and the booster.

The chicken wire cage was put in place and ready for the cotton.

The cotton was painted (airbrushed) lightly with yellow and grey/black before placed on the diorama base.

The wires from the lamp are hidden inside the smoke.

The background was a painted cardboard

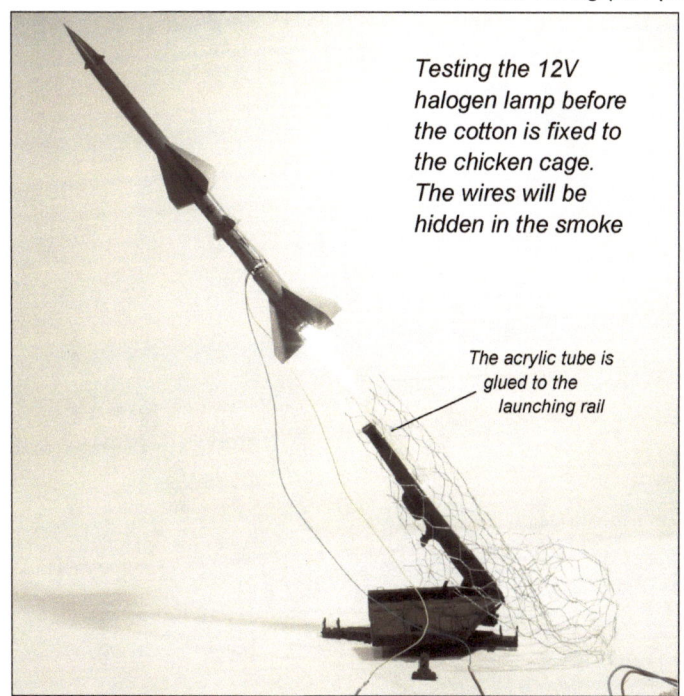

*Testing the 12V halogen lamp before the cotton is fixed to the chicken cage. The wires will be hidden in the smoke*

*The acrylic tube is glued to the launching rail*

*The cotton is in place. But not yet airbrushed with colour.
The wires are hidden In the smoke*

*The SA-2 missile in position ready for launch*

*This picture was taken before the acrylic tube, the light, the chicken wire and the cotton was put in place*

I made just one model of the SA-2 missile. On some of the pictures, you will see that there are three missile launch pads. They are all the same missile launcher. The two missiles in the background are pictured in different positions and pasted on the main picture. The reason I placed several launch pads in one picture was that several the SA-2 were always launched at the same time.
For example, in the U-2 incident, thirteen SA-2 were launched at the American aircraft.
The houses in the diorama are made of cardboard and painted. The cotton which is used as smoke is airbrushed. You can clearly see the different colours: Light grey/brown at the top and darker at the bottom because sand and dirt are swirled up from the blast.

*The SA-2 missile is launched on the diorama base*

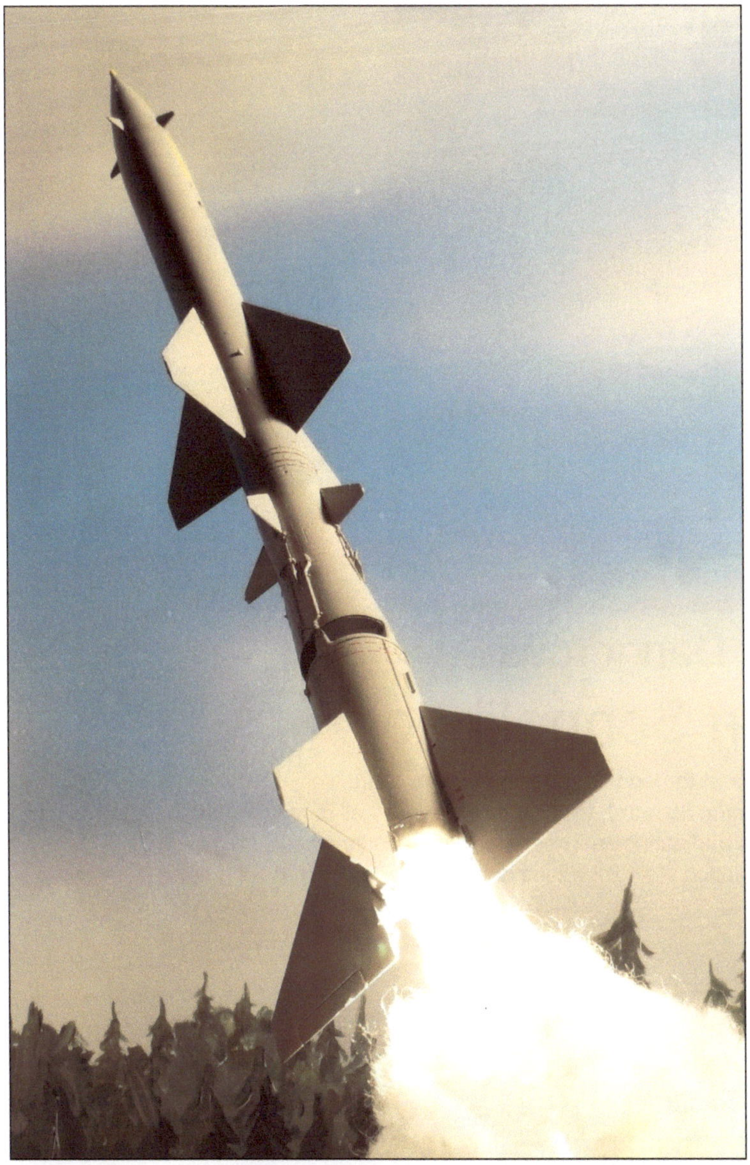
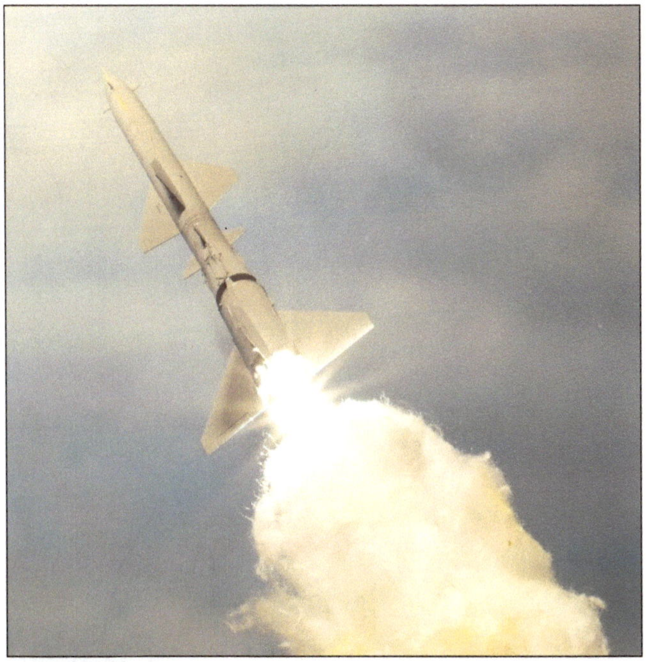
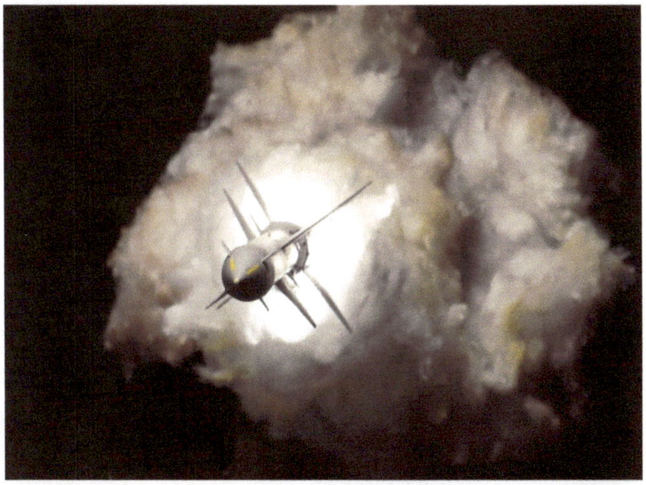
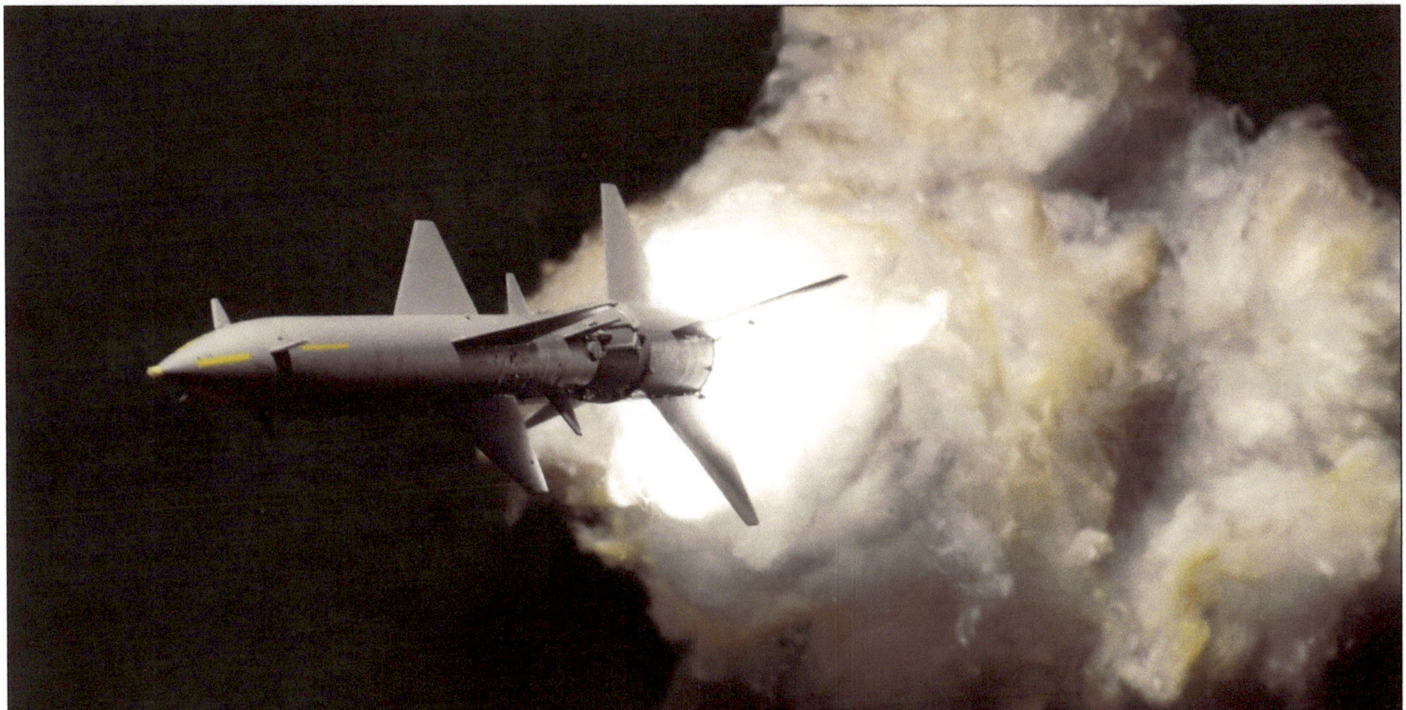

## Fast and Dangerous
# The German Schnellboot

The German Schnell Boats were the best torpedo boat designs of the entire war.
They were incredible fast (maximum speed 48 knots (89 km/h; 55 mph), they performed very well in rough seas, had great manoeuvrability and was heavily armed with torpedoes and cannons. They were a serious threat to all Allied ships.
They could emerge from the North Sea mist, launch their torpedoes and disappear just as quickly.

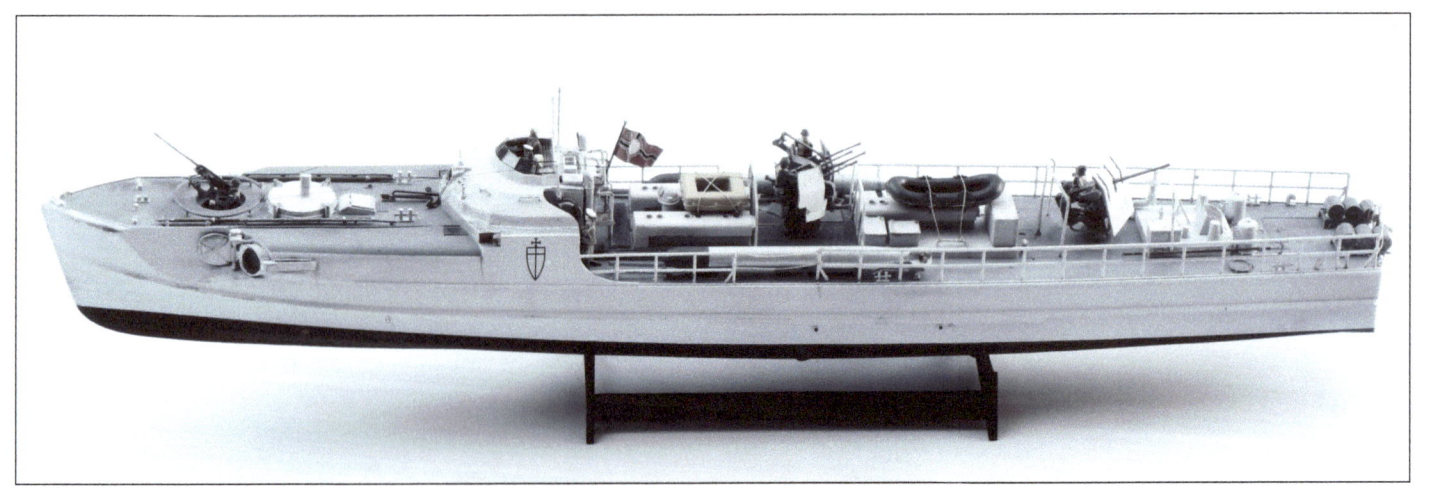

## Building the diorama

The "sea" was built on a Styrofoam plate 50 x 70 cm (20 x 33 in).

The S-boat in the diorama is going through the waves at full speed.
I made the bow-wave by a two component crystal resin which could be bent into the right shape before it hardened.

In retrospect, I am not sure this was necessary; I could probably have made the bow waves of paper Mache.

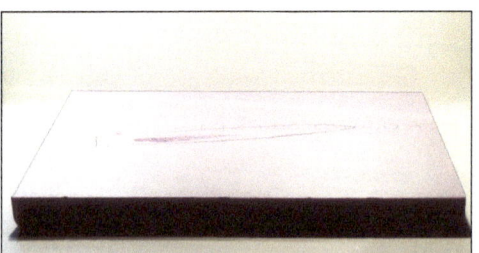

The sea and waves were made entirely of paper Mache. This is not difficult.
It's only a question of creativity and a sense of how a speedboat moves in the seas.
- I hope I got it a little bit right.
The pre-made bow waves by crystal resin were inserted in the paper Mache and the S-boat was placed in the Mache to make it easier to sculpt the waves made by the boat.
The model was wrapped in a plastic bag while placed into the wet paper Mache thus it could be removed without any damages or stain to the hull.
To create a believable sea spray was more tricky;
I tried to solve this problem by using a mix of "Water Effect", cotton and "Natural Water" from Woodland.
I hope I got the sea spray to look a little bit like sea spray, but I am not entirely satisfied with the result.
The painting of the sea is most important because it creates the atmosphere to the diorama - and is the most fun to do!
The S-boots operated mostly in the dark and the colours have to reflect this.
There is no blue sea in overcast and dark weather, the water is only grey and black (and maybe a little green), but the spray made by the boat and the wind is, of course, white.
All the painting was done by hand and with acrylic colours
After the fun of painting, it was time to wet the sea by using Natural Water from Woodland.
I only painted a thin layer of Natural Water on the whole base.

## The Background

I needed a background which would go with the dark sea and painted (on a cardboard) dark clouds and a burning ship for effect - the S-boot was after all engaged in an attack on enemy ships.

## The S-boat in daylight and fair weather

When I had photographed the S-boat in the dark seas, I would also present the model in clear daylight with blue sky and blue water. This was not the weather the S-boats liked the most, but I believe a beautiful boat as the S-302 needed to be seen in good weather.
I, therefore, let the wind calm a little (but not the waves), re-painted the sea and used one of my old backgrounds for a good-weather shooting.

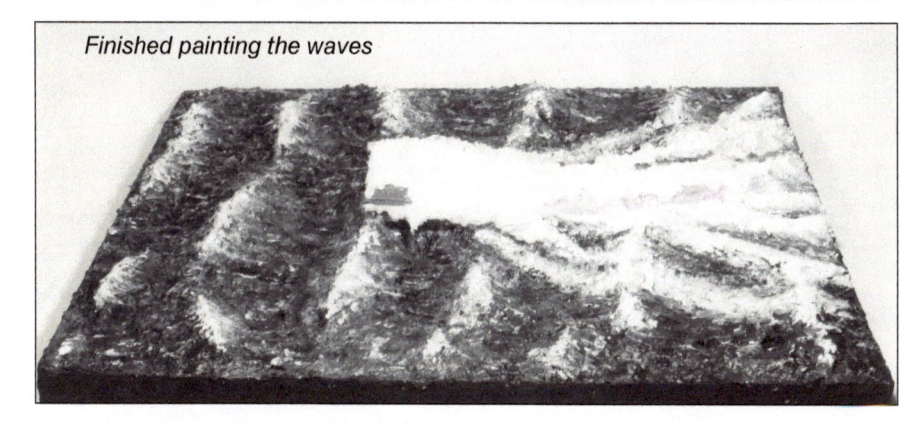

*Testing the fit of the boat in the waves*

*Painting the waves*

*Finished painting the waves*

*The boat in the dark night sea*

*The boat in the daylight sea*

98

99

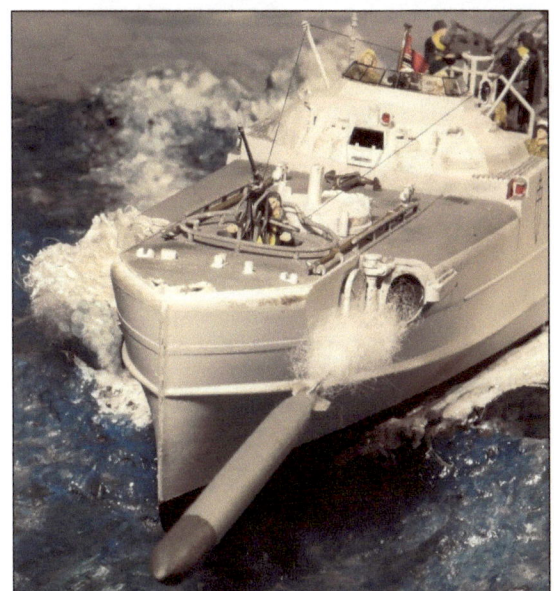

# Drama in Kattegat May 1940

## The Submarine

Early on the 4th May 1940, Captain Rupert Lonsdale sailed HMS Seal (37M), into Kattegat, the narrow strait between Denmark and Sweden. HMS SEAL was a big minelayer submarine. After laying the mines, the sub hit a German mine. No one was injured, but the rear part was damaged and SEAL took in about 130 tons of water and one of the diesel engines was damaged. After lying on the bottom until dark, Captain Lonsdale surfaced the submarine. They soon discovered that the rudders were destroyed by the explosion and the submarine was running in a circle. In desperation, they tried to reverse the submarine towards Sweden.

## The Sea Plane

At 02:00 May 5th, two Ar196 seaplanes took off from their base in Aalborg. Their mission was to patrol the sea between Skagen and the Swedish coast. Flying at only 50meter, one of the planes suddenly saw a shadow on the starboard side. In the semi-darkness, they could clearly see a submarine tower! The sub had the bow high in the water and the stern hidden under water and seems to be heading east towards Sweden. The crew in the Arado realised that the sub had to be British and attacked with two small bombs and machine guns. After a couple of attacks, the seaplane was out of ammunition and headed for shore.
At the same time, the other Arado appeared and started to attack the sub. After the second attack, this aircraft was also out of ammunition but continued to circle the sub.
On the submarine, the captain and crew were convinced that SEAL was about to sink. Lonsdale gave orders to bring up a white tablecloth from the mess and hoisted it in the mast as a sign of surrendering.

The pilot in the Ar196 could not believe his eyes when he saw the white flag!
He landed the plane, taxed to the submarine and demanded that the captain should swim to the plane and surrender! Soon afterwards the submarine captain jumps in the water and swam to the plane, crawled up on the float and was helped into the cockpit.

**It is this moment that is presented in the diorama**

*HMS Seal being towed to Fredrikshavn (Denmark) by German trawlers. You can still see the white tablecloth in the mast.*

*Above: German navy officers studying the marks from the Ar 196s machine guns. In fact, the attack from the small planes did not hurt de big submarine at all.*
*The listing to starboard was caused by the damage from the German mine and subsequent intake of water.*

# HMS SEAL

On the diorama, HMS SEAL is listing to starboard. The hull behind the tower is under water. The Ar196 have manoeuvred close to the submarine to take the captain POW.

I decided to build the diorama in scale 1:48.
This might be a problem because the sub was huge! 90m (296ft) means nearly 1.90m (74in) in 1:48. But since more than half of the sub is submerged, I might pull this off anyway.

Building the SEAL was a challenge. The submarine had to be built completely from scratch with whatever I had at hand: Plastic, styrene, putty and parts from all kind of old kits (most useful are a German Submarine kit in 1:72 and a small German coastal submarine kit in 1:48). But most of all, I had to rely on the drawings of SEAL and a lot of improvisation.

I used polystyrene as a cord for the hull. The shape is long and narrow with a marked narrowing in the middle of the foredeck.
I start by glueing 1mm (3/64in) styrene plates on the sides of the submarine.
The tower was made partly of parts from the kit of the German coastal submarine XXIII, styrene plates and pieces from old kits. The building was based on photos of SEAL

The gun position in front of the tower was entirely made of plastic pieces from old kits.
Much of the deck was taken from the German submarine kit, but much was also scratch built. There was a lot of filling and sanding before the transition between deck and hull were good.

I followed the ship drawings as close as possible and I think the result was reasonably similar to SEAL. Then the submarine crew was made, painted and glued in place, some in the tower and some on the deck, waving white tablecloths as a sign of surrender.
I found no British sailors in 1/48 and I had to adjust and change the figures I already had.

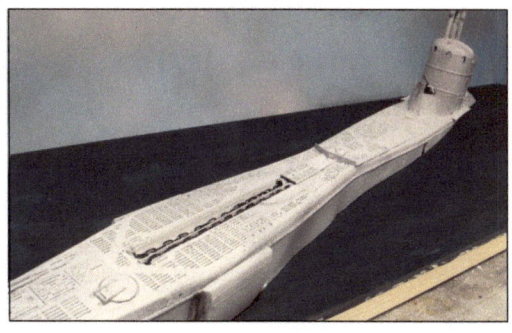

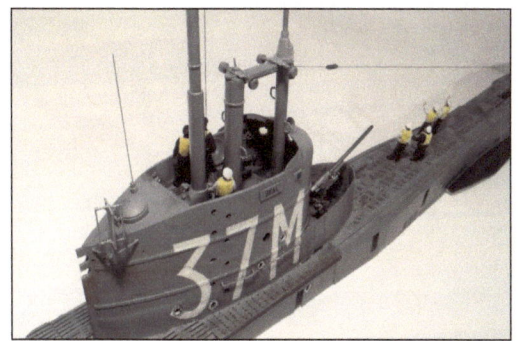

*The first "sketch" with dummy models*

101

# The Arado Ar 196

The aircraft is painted in RML 72/73/65 which was the standard camouflage for German seaplanes. This paint was relatively glossed in contrast to the paint on land-based aircraft.
Then three of the drama's main characters are placed in the Ar196:
Submarine Captain Lonsdale: Soaking wet and just wearing sweaters and trousers, enter the float after swimming to the small aircraft.
Pilot Lt.z.S. Schmidt: Trying to keep the plane into the wind as close to the submarine as possible while he communicates with Lonsdale. Observer Uffz. Sackritz: Manning the machine gun, keeping the crew at bay.

It is important that the propeller on the Ar196 looks like it's spinning. I used "PropBlur", which is a thin brass plate sculpted as a rotating propeller.
By painting it light grey, it can actually impose as a spinning propeller. The 6W+EN did not have a spinner and I had to throw away the spinner in the kit and make my own propeller hub.

The SEAL is now glued to the base and the ocean around the submarine is to be created. For this, I use paper Mache. It's easy to work with and has good adhesion to the surface, best of all it is easy to sculpt.
Then the water and the sea spray are painted with ordinary acrylic paint. To give the sea a "wet" look, I use the Woodland Scenics "Realistic Water".

I have made room for the sea plane's float in the waves and painted sea spray, caused by the propeller, where the front of the aircraft would be.

In the back of the diorama, I plan to put a cardboard plate to get more depth and reality. On the cardboard, I painted sea, dark clouds and the second Ar196 (6W+IN) in the air, circling the sub.
It is very early in the morning, just before sunrise, so the atmosphere is a little dark and intimidating.

At last, the Arado Ar196 6W+EN was glued to the sea and the diorama was finished!

The submarine was glued to the base and papier Mache was used to sculpt the waves.

The SEAL diorama is on display at Ålborg Maritime Museum (DK) It was here the German Seaplanes was based, and here the British Captain was brought in after surrendering. After the war, Captain Lonsdale was brought to court in Britain for having surrendered SEAL to the enemy. He was acquitted of all charges.

103

*The cannon on the deck was never used. Instead, the submarine crew used two Lewis machine guns mounted at the top of the tower and returned fire when the seaplanes attacked.
It did not take long before both machine guns jammed and became useless. After this, the submarine was virtually defenceless and surrendered to the two small German aircraft.*

The picture above is from a German propaganda film and shows three flags in the mast of SEAL: The German Kriegsmarine, the White Tablecloth and the British Ensign

105

# Blohm & Voss BV 138 refuelling at the Norwegian Arctic coast (1944)

The BV138 was a fascinating seaplane. Build to withstand rough arctic weather and stay airborne for 18 hours. It was powered by three 880hp diesel engines and could rendezvous with German subs in the middle of the Atlantic to refuel with diesel. It could master waves at 2,5 meter (12ft) and wind of 12m/s. And the BV 138 was by no means defenceless: One 20mm MG151 cannon in nose turret, one 20mm in the hull tail and one 13mm in open position after the central engine, plus six 50kg bombs. It had a crew of six.

The BV138 was operating from the northern Norwegian coast until the end of the war. One of its main tasks was shadowing Allied convoys to Murmansk and Archangelsk and lead the German submarines to the convoys.

The aircraft in the diorama had its main base in Trondheim, but it also had to manage with rather primitive secondary bases along the particularly exposed North Norwegian Arctic coast. In the diorama, the BV138 has landed at a small fishing community to refill diesel.

The diorama is happening sometime during the winter of 1944.

I have tried to make the diorama as authentic "North Norwegian" as possible with the high (due to large tidal range) wooden dock and the typical red wooden housing.

All the diorama elements are in scale 1/48

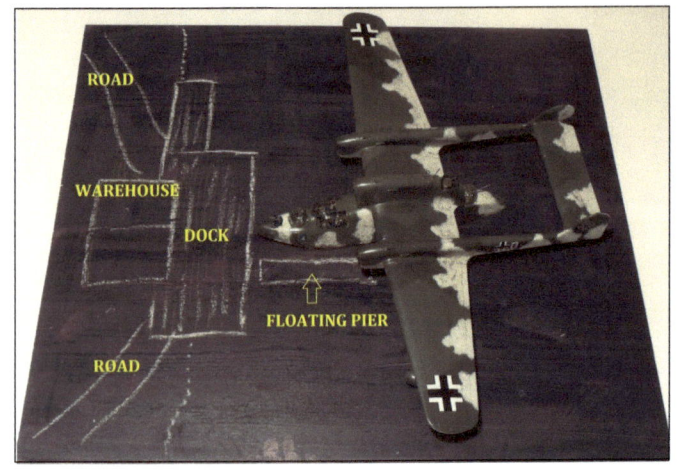

*The BV138-model used in the diorama*

## The sketch

I used a model of BV 138 which I already had made and painted in arctic snow camouflage, and which was operating in the far north.
I only had to prepare the model of the flying boat for "floating" in the water. This I did by sawing off the underwater fuselage.
The plane was a rather large plane, especially in 1/48 and the base had to be large as well. I found a wooden board of about 70x60cm (28"x24"), which would fit nicely. With the wooden board ready, I made a sketch of the diorama layout – the way I wanted it.
And then I had to build the dock, the warehouse, the landscape and the other bits and pieces to make the diorama believable and realistic.

# The Plane

First, I saw off the bottom of the hull and the floats by the waterline. Then I open the hatch in the nose of the fuselage. This hatch was used when mooring the plane. The same goes for the hatch at the rear end of the hull. I also had to open the hatch on the port side of the central nacelle to let the crew out for refilling diesel.

# The Propellers

The plane was lying at the dock and I had to remove the "PropBlurs" I had used for the "spinning propellers" on the model and replaced them with propeller blades.
Three blades propellers on the outer engines and four blades on the central engine

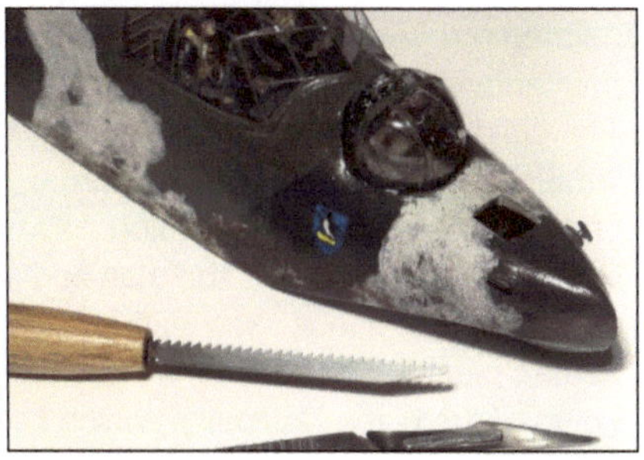

# The Rowboat

I decided I had to have a small rowboat alongside the plane so I made a typical Norwegian rowboat called a "pram" out of styrene sheets.

# The Dock

The dock had to be the typical wooden dock you will find all over North Norway
This was made from wooden spatulas and sticks, cut to sizes and glued together.
It was painted as a very weathered dock.

# The Crane

The dock had a crane to lift the heavy goods. This was made of styrene sheets and bits and pieces from old kits. It was painted rusty and "old", just like cranes I have seen in places like this.

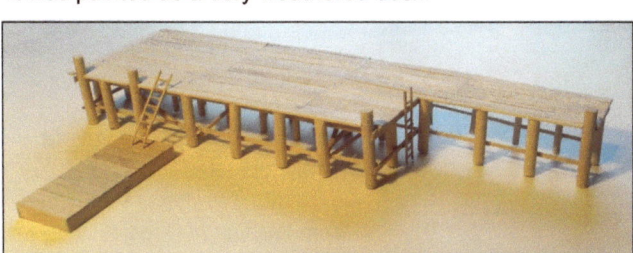

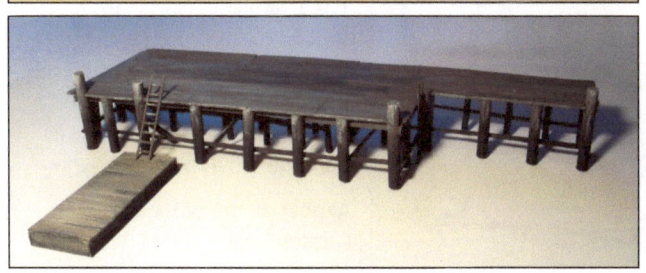

# The Warehouse

On the dock, it has to be a wooden warehouse typical for a fishing community in North Norway.
The Germans used this for storing diesel fuel and other necessities for the seaplanes. This kind of buildings (warehouses, barns etc.) was always painted red (red was the cheapest paint in previous times).
The building on the dock was highly weathered by the fierce arctic winters. I first made a cardboard building.
On this, I glued wooden spatulas and sticks to make it look like weather-beaten planks.
I named the place Naustvika, which I painted on the front of the building.

# The Base

Then it was time for the making the base. First, I glued Styrofoam to make the terrain behind the dock. Pebbles was glued to the slope down to the sea and some paper Mache was added to sculpt the snow-covered terrain. The dock and the warehouse and crane were glued in place. The sea was covered with a thin layer of paper Mache to make the impression of small ripples on the surface.
Then everything was painted with acryllic paint.

Then all the bits and pieces needed to make the diorama credible were made:
The ground crew, the diesel filling equipment and diesel barrels, the moorings, the fenders and so on and so on.

The ground crew is mostly made from Tamiya 1:48 German Maintenance Set but highly "adjusted" to fit the scenario. The bystanders are from Woodland Scenic.
The Refuelling Cart is from Verlinden.
The truck is a 1932 Ford (from UM), which I believe is requisitioned by the Germans from the local merchant.

Almost all the other stuff is scratch build

# The background

The last part to be made was the background which I painted on a cardboard. I chose a typical North Norwegian mountain landscape, which looked right in this setting. I used acrylic paint. The background is 100x70cm (40"x28") All the details in the diorama are in scale 1:48 and the total dimension are: 70x60cm (28"x24")

## When everything was put together the diorama looked like this:

109

110

The diorama is on display at TROMS DEFENCE MUSEUM in North Norway

The army co-op aircraft which became the famous SOE's "Spy-Taxi"
# The legendary "Lizzie"

## Westland Lysander

During the war, the Lysander was used in a variety of roles in different parts of the world but was best known for transporting spies and resistance fighters behind enemy lines in France. In this role, Lizzie performed well due to its extraordinarily short take-off and landing capacities, which was used whenever someone needed to be extracted from occupied France.

Lizzie operated in and out of unprepared fields, pastures, and forest clearings in the dark of night to pick-up secret agents and saboteurs.

To give it the long range it needed, the aircraft had to be lightened by removing all unnecessary equipment such as guns, armour protection and radio equipment, retaining only the radio-telephone for communication with the ground.

The pilot had to find his way by map, reading light, and the glow of a full moon.

A small field or a clearing in the woods would be sufficient for the Lizzie. Landing strips in France were marked out by four or five torches, hastily lit and doused as needed.

To slip in unobtrusively, the Lysanders were painted matte black.

**This diorama is a tribute to the brave SOE pilots in their Lizzies**

# The plane

The "Lizzie" I am building is the Lysander Mk III SCW (Special Contract Westland) which was the special version for clandestine operations.
All armament was removed from the plane and a long-range 150-gallon external fuel tank mounted underneath the aircraft.
An external ladder was mounted on the port side for easy access to the passenger cockpit.
The aircraft was painted all black by hand (no airbrush).
The figures were something I found in my scrapping box.

# The Propeller

I needed the propeller to rotate and had to use the brass rod/brass tube method where the "propeller shaft" runs in a brass tube and everything lubricated with dry graphite lubricant. With this method, the propeller will spin with the slightest wind (I used a hair dryer). The prop to the right in the picture to the left are running at full throttle.

# The Base

As a base for the diorama, I used an old one I had made for a tank diorama, made of a wooden base covered with paper Mache, painted, and covered with static grass and decorated with trees and bushes mostly found in my back yard.

I made a new background by painting a dark sky and some backdrop of tree silhouettes.
Everything painted in acrylic colours

On the next pages,
I let the diorama and the pictures tell the story of "Lizzie" and the SOE pilots flying to France at night, delivering SOE-agents and extracting resistant fighters from Nazi occupation.

Above:
Preparing for the night's flight into enemy territory. The last briefing before take-off.

Left:
Flying low over France without armament or radio to find their way to the secret destination.
The moonlight and a roadmap were the only means the pilot had to find their way to the rendezvous.

Below:
… a clearing in the woods – and torches - yes, we found you!
Landing strips were usually marked out by four or five torches, hastily lit and doused as needed.

The pictures above and to the right are made by pasting pictures of the model into different backgrounds.
The background pictures are either my own pictures or images I find on the net.

On the picture to the right, the fires and the waiting personnel have been pasted on the background as well as the plane.

The propeller is spinning by the help of a little wind from a hairdryer

Exchange of SOE operatives and saboteurs. Every minute counts. The Germans might be nearby.

Lizzie was designed to carry one passenger in the rear cockpit, but for SOE use, the rear cockpit was modified to carry two passengers.

In extreme situations, they could squeeze in three passengers – very uncomfortable – but it got'em back to safety.

Thanks to the extreme STOL capacity, the Lysanders could land and start in rough terrain and very short distances, a small field or a clearing in the woods would be sufficient for the Lizzie.

The SOE Lysanders were fitted with a fixed ladder on the port side to provide quick access to the rear cockpit.

A large fuel tank under the belly provided enough fuel to get Lizzie back to Britain

Take-off as quickly as possible, hoping they were not spotted by the Germans.

115

# Hanna Reitsch: Hitler's Female Test pilot

## The Story

On April 26, 1945, Hanna Reitsch was in the narrow cockpit of a small Fieseler Fi-156C Storch together with Luftwaffe Generaloberst Ritter von Greim.
Underneath was Berlin, burning and completely encircled by the Russian armies. They planned to persuade Hitler to fly out with them and escape to Bavaria.
von Greim was flying the small STOL reconnaissance aircraft and Hanna crouched behind him.
Flying low over the burning city and through a hail of Soviet anti-aircraft fire, the plane was hit in the engine and fuel tank. An armour-piercing bullet hit von Greim's right foot, and he passed out. How Hanna managed to take control of the Storch is short of a miracle.
The seats in the Fi-156 are placed behind each other and there is no room to get around the seats. With the pilot unconscious, there is normally no space to switch places – but the person in the back seat was a small woman (5 ft) and she managed to crawl over to the front seat, take control of the plane and continued towards the centre of Berlin.
The Fi-156 needed no more than 21m (70ft) of landing space, but the streets in Berlin was filled with demolished houses, wrecks and barricades. There was hardly any place to land, but Hanna managed to put the Storch down on the war beaten boulevard near Brandenburger Tor. During intense Russian bombardment, both made it to Hitler's bunker, where they stayed for two days.
But Hitler would not listen to their pleading and refused to leave the bunker. On the 28th April, Hitler ordered them to flee Berlin and in the final hours of the Russian assault on the city, von Greim and Reitsch escaped in an aircraft (an Arado Ar 96) hidden near the bunker.

She was the last person to get out of the beleaguered Berlin.

Two days later, Hitler committed suicide and the war was over.

*Hanna Reitsch, the famous German female pilot. She died in Frankfurt in 1979*

*Brandenburger Tor, May 1945. It was near this place that Hanna Reitsch landed with the small Fieseler Storch on April 26, 1945*

**The diorama shows the Fieseler Storch and the two pilots on the ground at the Brandenburger Tor while the war rages around them and German soldiers desperately try to stem the Soviet army.**

# The famous Brandenburger Tor

Brandenburger Tor will be part of the background in this diorama.

As you can see from the picture taken after the war, (see the previous page), the place in front of the famous Gate was not in the best state. When Hanna Reitsch landed there, it was obviously much worse with intense bombardment from the Soviet Armies all around - and closing in.

The building of the Gate was easy enough, just some wooden sticks as columns and cardboard and Polystyrene as building material for everything else.

All were painted with acrylic colours. The damages were extensive; it was a wonder the Gate was still standing while most of the surrounding buildings were just piles of rubbish.

I painted a dark smoke-filled background of a burning city.

The lights in the background in the diorama are ordinary battery-operated Christmas deco lights.

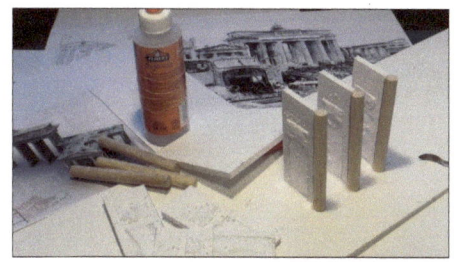

# Hanna Reitsch and von Greim

I had to make the two main characters in this drama out of bits and pieces of 1:48 figures in my toolbox.

von Greim was wounded in his right foot and after he had gained consciousness after the landing, Hanna had to help him on their way to the Führerbunker which was not far from Brandenburger Tor.

*Above: The rear entrance to the Führerbunker. It was not far from here that the Ar 96 (trainer), which they used to escape from Berlin, was hidden.*

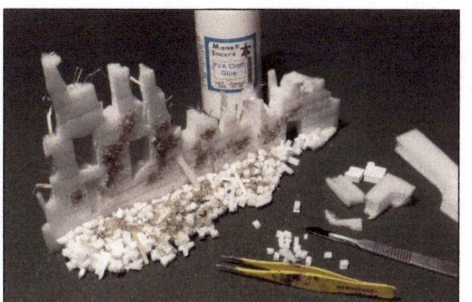

# The Props

At the Boulevard in front of Brandenburger Tor, there would be all kind of debris, ruins, soldier, burned out vehicles etc.
I built and painted some Wehrmacht soldiers, a bullet-ridden Sd.Kfz.10 German half-track and a Citroen staff car plus a damaged, but still working Flak 30 (20mm) canon.

117

# Fieseler Fi-156C Storch

The picture to the right is the only picture of Hanna's Fi-156 which I have found.
It shows the Storch placed behind the Brandenburger Tor, guarded by a British soldier (you can see the Siegessäule in the background).

The plane was badly damaged when the picture was taken. In addition to the damages inflicted by Soviet AAA, it was most likely hit several times when parked on the ground. And obviously, souvenir looters also had a field day before the picture was taken.

The plane on the picture is therefore not representative.

If fact, the Storch went through an unbelievable barricade of Soviet AAA.
They were lucky. Normally; a slow flying plane like the Storch should never have reached its destination.

The plane received several hits in the wings and fuselage which tore up the skin (fabric) in several places, but the plane could still fly.

The fuel tank (in the wing) was hit, so was the engine cowling and some panels were ripped off.
To get it as authentic as possible, I had to build all these damages into the model.
For the visual damages, I made some holes both in the upper and lower wings, made new wing beams of styrene (which could be seen in the openings) and used thin metal sheets to substitute for the torn fabric in the wings.

The metal sheets were borrowed from a tube of Bacon Cheese.

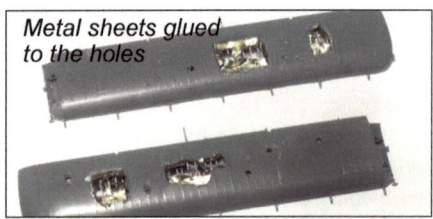

*New wing beams of Styrene*

*The new wing beams shows through the holes*

*Metal sheets glued to the holes*

*Painted with primer*

The diorama is about 61 x 70 cm (27 x 30 ins) and will be on display at the new WWII hanger at East Midlands Aeropark (UK)

119

## My first diorama

I do not have this diorama anymore; it is on display at East Midlands Aeropark (UK). But I have the pictures, which was not taken for the purpose of being published, but I think this diorama is a good example of how to make a diorama with creativity and very little experience.

I had never made a diorama before, but I wanted to try and see what I could manage and looked at some web sites to get some ideas how to do this.
I wanted to make a crash landing and had a 1/48 Bf 109G from JG27 that I made some time ago. I thought it would be nice to use this aircraft in a crash diorama.
First, I needed a base and found an old picture in glass and frame which I thought could do. On the framed picture, I put some plaster and sculpted it as the terrain.
Then I found an old green carpet with very short fibres. The problem was that the fibres looked synthetic and not as grass. I had to change that.
I used a hot iron to make the rug look rough and uneven, brushed it with a steel brush and painted it with mat acrylic colours. When done, I glued it to the plaster.
It looked OK, but I needed some dirt, stones, gravel and bushes.
The stones, I found in my back yard and the bushes were made of twisting thin wires from the inside of an electrical lamp cable.

I bought some artificial grass from Woodland Scenics and sprinkled the terrain.
For longer grass, I cut some hair from an old paint brush and glued it on the ground.
I made a fence from tooth sticks and used a thin thread as wires between the poles.
The plane needed to look like it had belly landed in a rough field so I tore off the main wheels, used a candle to heat the propeller blades and bend the wing tip.
I ripped off the flaps on the port side, loosened the tail and wing rudders, opened the hatch on the fuselage port side and made bullet holes in the wings, fuselage and tail.
The plane was then glued to the ground, skid marks were made of plaster and painted, bits and pieces of the plane were left behind the plane and the canopy placed beside the fuselage.
Then I placed the pilot and some German soldiers outside the plane and glued on a Kübelwagen which I had made some time ago.

And that was it. To be honest, I was quite satisfied with my first diorama – and it hadn't cost me anything, except for the old models.
When I photographed the diorama, I used a wall decal mounted on a cardboard as background.

*Normal plaster on an old picture.*

*A green carpet was painted and made as rough as possible and glued to the plaster.*

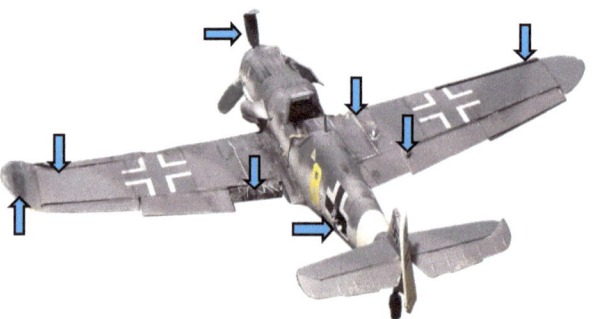

*Different parts of the aircraft that was damaged : The propeller blades, bent wingtip, flaps, tail, wing rudders, front of wings, open hatch in fuselage and bullets holes*

*Black/white photos: Trying to make the pictures look like old photos from the war.*

121

# Ju 88C-6 Zerstörer Crashlanding

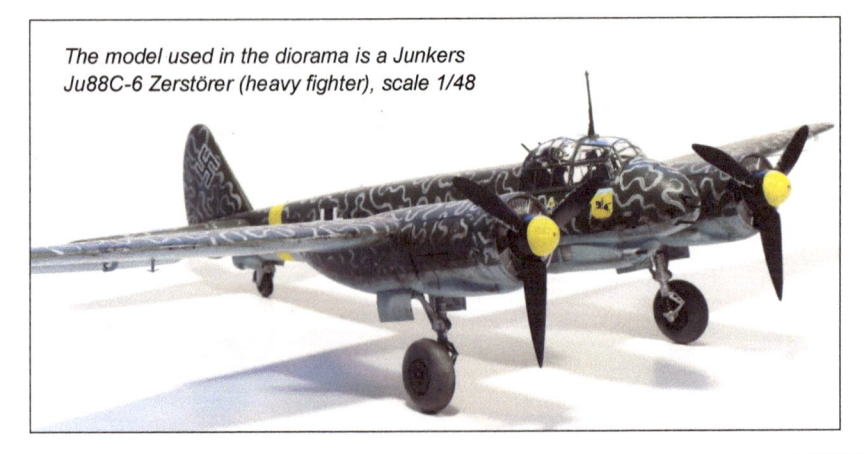

*The model used in the diorama is a Junkers Ju88C-6 Zerstörer (heavy fighter), scale 1/48*

## The story:

The Zerstörer was badly damaged by enemy fire, especially in the starboard wing and the tail section. The starboard engine started to burn and they had to make a forced landing.

The plane landed on its belly, lost speed and the starboard wing struck a tree.
The badly damaged wing broke off and the Zerstörer ended up in a small creek.

The fire ceased to burn and the crew escaped with minor injuries. Shortly after, German soldiers arrived.

## The diorama

The diorama is built around a crashed Ju88 (scale 1/48). The plane was made some time ago and was collecting dust on a shelf. I thought it was time to do something more exciting with the model.

As always, I started with a sketch of how I wanted the diorama. The base for the diorama was a wooden plate 60 x 40 cm (24"x16").
For moulding the terrain, I used some polyethene packaging material which I roughly cut to make the terrain and the river. I also found an old green carpet, which was used as the base for grass, trees and bushes, it just needed to be painted.
Stones, gravel and sand for the river bed, was right in my back yard. It was just to pick what I needed.

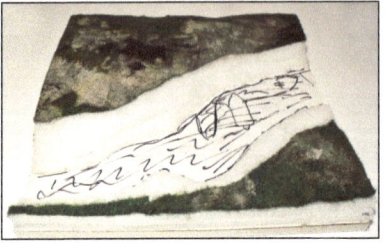

# The Plane

The first I did to the model was to rip and saw off all the parts which were damaged or destroyed during the landing:
The starboard wing, the rudders, the propellers, the engine covers, the canopy, the landing gear, the starboard nacelle etc.

I put a new Junkers Jumo 211 engine into the starboard nacelle and painted it black and burned.
Broken wires and tubes were placed in the nacelle to make it as realistic as possible.
Very thin metal sheets were used as the skin of the aircraft and bent like it was part of an explosion.

The nacelle and part of the wing were painted badly burned.

The sawed-off wing and the wing beams in front and in the back of the wing were issued with a perforated strut.
The wings on a plane are incredibly strong and I needed some badly damages to justify the rip-off of the wing.
Therefore, holes after cannon shell were made in the wing and especially near the wing beams.

The plane was also hit in the tail and the stabilizers. I made holes and shredded metal skins accordingly.

The landing flaps on the starboard side were partly ripped apart but were hanging onto the outer wing.

The wing beams were clearly visible extending from the broken wing.
The propellers were heated over a candle and bent backwards.

I use drawings of the plane to get everything as correct as possible.

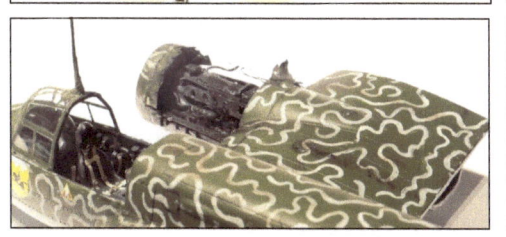

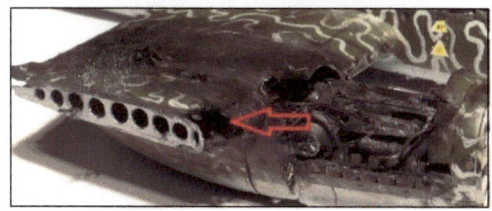

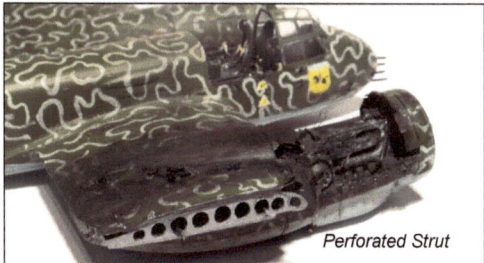

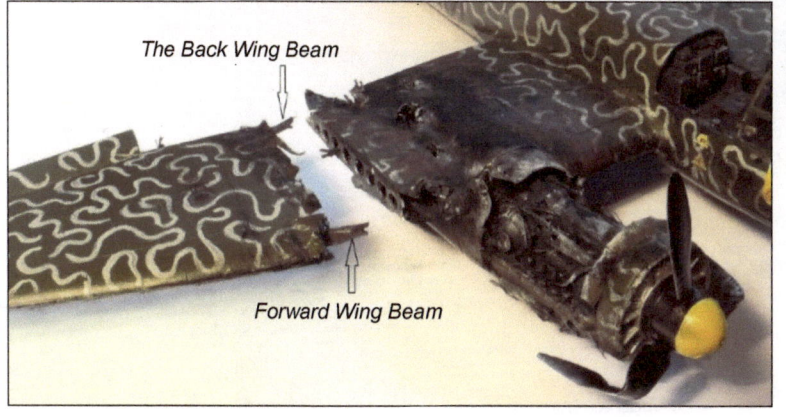

*The plane was ripped apart*

*A new engine placed in the nacelle*

*Perforated Strut*

*The Back Wing Beam*

*Forward Wing Beam*

123

# Trees and Bushes

The trees were made by twisting wires (from a lamp cord) around a wooden stick. By twisting the wires into smaller parts, you can make the branches of the tree, as many and as thin as you would like. This is a technique which is good when making bushes and smaller trees. To get the stem as natural as possible, I used clear School Glue, mixed with sawdust. Where do you get sawdust? Try a saw and a piece of wood.

The small branches had to be airbrushed, otherwise, it is almost impossible to paint all the thin wires.

To get the leaves on the tree, I sprayed it with hairspray to get the branches sticky, then sprinkle it with artificial grass.

It adheres to the hairspray and with a sympathetic look, it could be leaves. This is an easy way to make trees and bushes with very little effort – and at very little cost!

All the trees and bushes in this diorama are made this way.

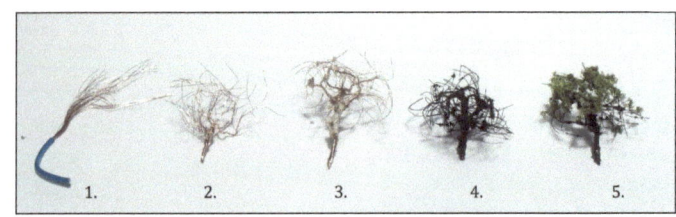

# The Vehicle

The help arrived in an armoured half-track personnel carrier, Sd.Kfz.251/1, in short, 251

This APC could carry a crew of two and up to ten infantrymen. The Soldiers took care of the wounded aircraft crew and formed a perimeter around the crash site.

I have also placed a couple of civilian onlookers on the other side of the creek. It is probably an old farmer and his dog, together with his war-injured son.

# The Diorama

125

## Messerschmitt Bf109 E-7 Trop
# Crash landing in the Libyan Desert

The Bf109s from JG27 (Jagdgeswader) was synonymous with the Afrika Korps and the campaign in North Africa. The JG 27 provided Rommel's army with fighter protection for virtually the whole 'roller coaster ride that was the war in the Libyan Desert from 1941-43. The JG27 was formed in 1939 and saw considerable action both during the Battles of France and Britain.

JG 27 was sent to North Africa in April 1941 and the Geschwader had an immediate impact on the campaign, which had up until then been dominated by the Allied.

Fighting against the Desert Air Force's generally inferior Hawker Hurricanes and Curtiss P-40s, which were often flown by inexperienced and under-trained pilots. The German Bf 109s inflicted heavy losses, although serviceability in the harsh conditions and chronic fuel shortages greatly reduced the effectiveness of the Geschwader.

The famous Hans-Joachim Marseille was the JG27's top ace.

## The Diorama

The diorama shows one of the JG 27 aircraft shot down over the Libyan Desert in 1941. It is nothing dramatic about this incident - I just felt like making a desert diorama. The pilot managed to put the plane down in more or less one piece and was picked up without any major injuries by a German patrol. The day after, he was probably in the air again, fighting the Hurricanes and P-40's

# The patrol car and the German soldiers

The car was a 1/35 scale German Steyr from Deutsches Afrika-korps (the German Africa Corps).
The colour was light brown/yellow – very close to the colour of the Libyan Desert.
The figures are a mix of old figures used in other dioramas plus a couple of new from the Steyr-kit.
The pilot was obvious a little groggy, but unhurt and taken good care of by the German soldiers.

# Building the base

To make the base, I used a 50x50cm (20x20 inches) Styrofoam plate I found in my garage.
Then I used a hand saw to shape the top of the Styrofoam the way I wanted the desert floor and painted the outline of the aircraft to see how it might look.
The next step was to cover the base with a thin layer of paper Mache and use some small stones, some pebbles and some sand to create the desert surface.
I used thinned paper glue to bind the sand to the paper Mache.
The next step was to paint the base.
The Libyan Desert is rather colourful with orange/yellow/red sand. I mixed acrylic paint until I had a colour I felt was right.
For the painting of bases, I always use cheap cans of acrylic paint bought in a hobby shop or a hardware. I always use a hand brush because hand brushing allows me to make different shades of colours, which I can't do with an airbrush.
The paint was thinned and hand brushed to the sand and stones.
And last, I placed some bushes on the diorama, mostly for decoration.
The background is just a piece of cardboard on which I painted a blue sky and sand dunes.

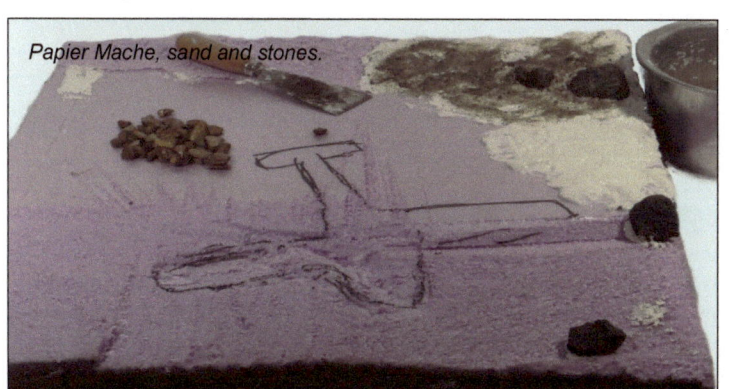

*The crash was obviously well behind enemy lines and the atmosphere was therefore quite relaxed.*

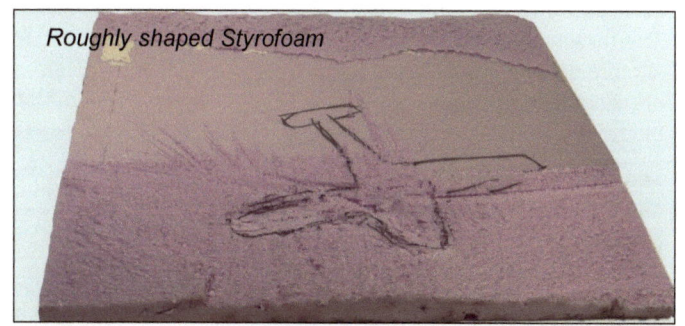

*Roughly shaped Styrofoam*

*Papier Mache, sand and stones.*

*Painted with acrylic paint*

127

# Making damages to the Bf109 Trop

I used a 1/32 model of a Bf 109 Trop which I had made a couple of years ago in another setting.

Now, it was just collecting dust on a shelf and was brought back to life as the «Yellow 4» in this diorama.

The plane was originally painted in colours used in Europe, and I had to repaint it and give it a typical desert camouflage.

When the plane crash landed in the desert, it had, of course, several damages, some from the air battle with enemy fighters and some from the belly-landing on the rough desert floor.

As always, the plastic in the model is far too thick to be used to create realistic damages in the aircraft skin. The thickness of the plastic in a model is more suitable for a tank, and not for creating authentic damages on an aircraft.

I needed far thinner skin and made several holes in the model on which I glued thin metal sheets as a new skin. I also changed a couple of the engine panels with thin metal sheets to look like they were loosened during the rough landing.

The metal I used was taken from a tube of mayonnaise which I liberated from the fridge - easy and very inexpensive.

I have been using this technique several times and it's always very efficient to create realistic damages on an aircraft.
The metal is cut into suitable sizes and glued to the damaged part of the aircraft by CA-glue. It is easy to correct the metal bits by just using a small scissor.
When all the bits and pieces are in place, the metal is painted in the aircraft colour.

In the rudder and stabilisers, I drilled holes where the canvas had been ripped off.

The aircraft had belly landed and the main undercarriages were still intact in the wings.

*Above: Holes - big and small - are made in the fuselage and tail (by drill and a sharp knife)*

*Above: Thin metal sheets cut with a scissor are glued to the holes and bent to fit.*

*Above: The metal bits are painted in the aircraft colour and look quite authentic on the model. Below: Note the panels in front of the cockpit and see how much more lifelike the metal sheet are compared to the much thicker plastic in the kit. The propeller blades are warmed by a candle and bent backwards.*

The old Bf 109 model was repainted, new decals were applied, a little weathering was put on and I had a bona fide crash-landed Messerschmitt operating in Libya during World War 2

If you noticed, I chose to leave the canopy intact after the landing.

From pictures I have seen from such landings in WWII, some pilots ejected the hinged canopy before landing.

This was a precaution if the plane should end upside-down and the canopy could not be opened.

If the pilot in a Bf109 chooses to eject the canopy, the rear part of the canopy would also be gone.

I let my pilot belong to those who landed with the canopy in place (besides I think it looks better that way), but the hinges were broken in the rough landing and the mid part of the canopy fell down when it was opened by the pilot.

→ I have indicated by arrows the damages I have done to the aircraft.

129

Waiting for the rescue team

131

# B-17 Crash Landing

For this diorama, I used a B-17 from the 100th Bomb Group which I made some years ago. The model (1:48) was not intended for a diorama but I felt that it might be ideal for making a realistic crash diorama and I was prepared to ruin my nice model (!)

Below you can see the original model standing on the hardstand (diorama) at the 100th BG base at Thorpe Abbots in Norfolk (England) – the buildings in the background are just part of the backdrop. The crew is ready for the bomb mission deep into Germany.

*This picture was made by pasting a picture of the model into a new background.*
*The spinning propellers are achieved by blowing at the aircraft with a hairdryer*

# The Aircraft

Looking at pictures of battle damaged B-17 gave me an idea of the kind of damages I had to inflict on the plane.

The damages had to be realistically, believable and extensive enough for the plane to struggle its way back to England. The plane was already painted and weathered so it was just for me to start making holes in the fuselage and wings caused by exploding Flak grenades and 20mm cannon shells from German fighters.

Of course, the aircraft skin of a plastic model is far too thick to be realistic. The thickness of the plastic is between 1,5 and 2mm, which correspond to about 8cm (3,2") in scale. There is no way this thickness would look anything like normal. I, therefore, glued thin sheets of metal on the sides of the holes. For this, I used the metal from a tube of mayonnaise (sponsored by my wife). The metal sheets were then painted in the aircraft colour. The holes in the aircraft also exposed the structure underneath the aluminium skin and this structure had to be made by the help of styrene sheets cut out to fit the damage.

The rudders were covered with "silver dope" over an aluminium skeleton and the holes here had to be treated differently than the holes in the aluminium covered fuselage. I used paper strips to give the illusion of fabric around the holes in the rudders.

The engine fire had also set its mark on the starboard wing and balance rudder, which of course was highly stained by smoke from the burning engine.

*Starting with a perfectly good model, every opening I cut out of the fuselage or wings had to be treated basically the same way: Glueing thin sheets of metal on the edges of the opening, putting in spants or frames (made of styrene) when necessary and painting everything in the aircraft colours*

The damages to the fuselage are good examples of the technique I used. Large parts of the fuselage skin were blown away and spants were bent or broken. Obviously, a shell had exploded inside the aircraft and blown big holes in the fuselage. The thin aircraft skin was forced backwards by the airstream. The front had partly been torn apart, Plexiglas chattered and fuselage ripped open.

It's no less than unbelievable to see the damages these big bombers could sustain – and still be flying.

Above:
The styrene sheets are cut in suitable sizes and formed as spants and ribs. Then they are placed in the open damaged part in the tail and fuselage section and painted.

Above and to the right:
Holes are cut in the rudders to look like the dope is partly removed, thin metal sheets are glued to the openings and everything are painted.
CA-glue is used to fix the metal to the plastic.

## All the damages are now done and the B17 is ready for the crash site

# The Base

Before I started, I needed an idea for how the diorama should be, and I made a mental sketch:

The plane ended on a grassy field and skidded along until it came to a standstill quite near a dirt road, which made it easy for the recovery vehicles to quickly reach the downed plane.

I chose not to have any fancy buildings in the diorama, but concentrate on the necessary and realistic surroundings.

I used chipboard as a base for the diorama.

I painted both sides so it would stay flat and not curve due to moisture from any wet stuff I put on the plate.

Second, I build up some terrain with the help of more chipboard and Styrofoam and then covered everything with paper Mache.

The whole surface was painted to give a coloured base for static grass

*The idea*

*The chipboard*

*The Paper Mache*

*Painting the base with acryl*

*Adding static grass*

*Bushes and trees*

# The Vehicles

I used the following vehicles (all in 1:48 scale): A Jeep, a Dodge WC54 Ambulance and two 2 1/2- Ton Cargo Trucks which I scratch build to be a fire/rescue truck and a Wrecker Truck.

135

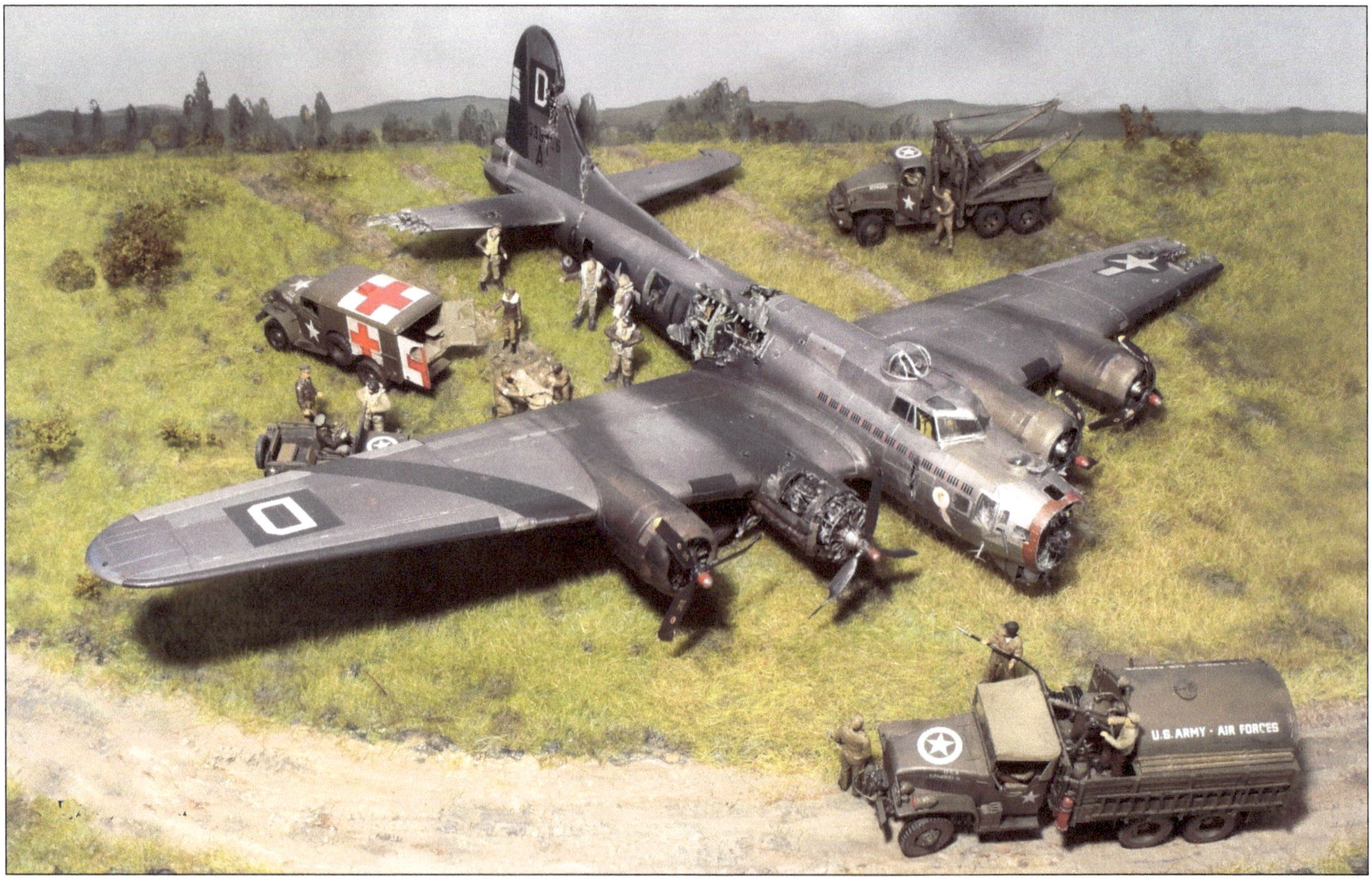
D
U.S. ARMY - AIR FORCES

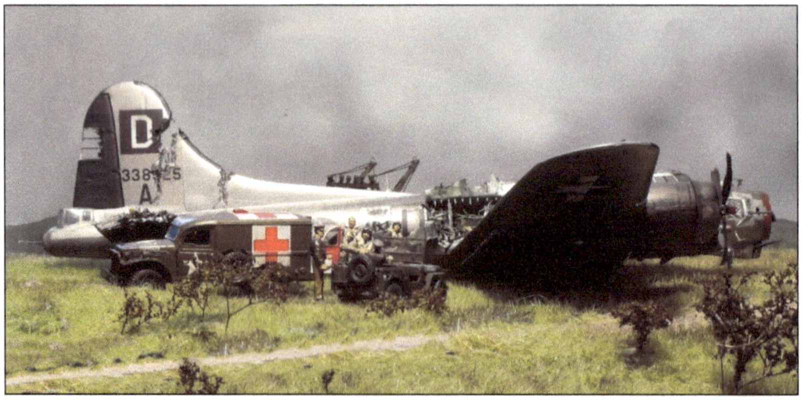
D

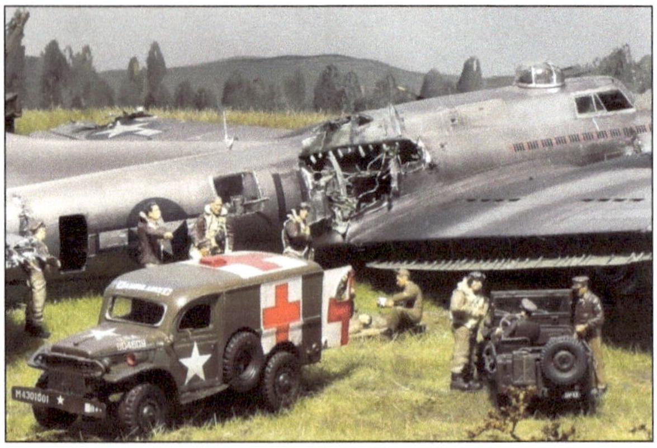

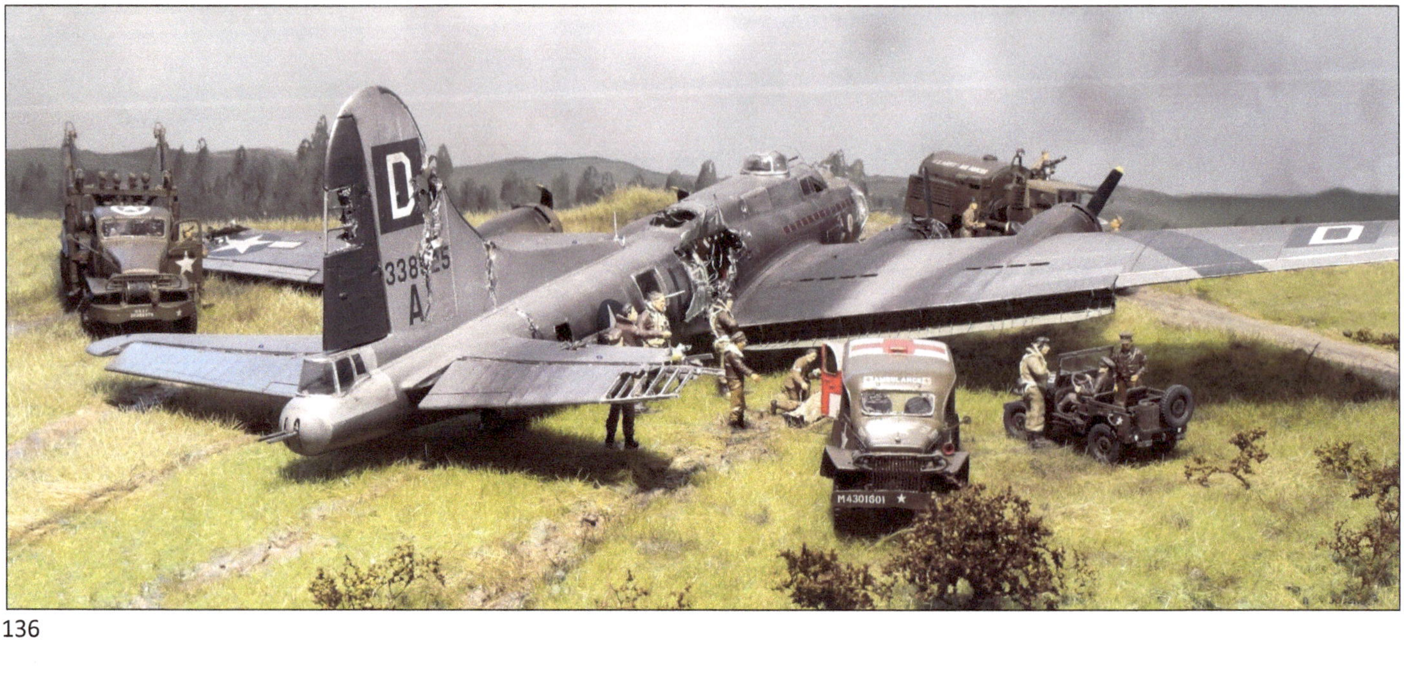
D
A

137

## To tell a story:

I very much like to let my models tell a story. It brings more life to the models and is challenging to me as a model maker. And it's fun to look at. Maybe even uses it at a framed picture.

The picture to the right for example:
The B17 has been hit hard and tries to reach home base with one engine burning. I created this picture with using a photo editing program to "paint" smoke from the burning engine. The background is a painted cardboard. It's very easy to do this, and the result is often rather dramatic.
**More examples on the next page.**

# Taking Pictures

I feel that pictures of a model in its natural environment are essential to a presentation. I always try to make the pictures as lifelike and realistic as possible and I have often been asked how I do it. It has been written books about this subject, but in reality, it's rather simple.

What you need is a camera where you can manually adjust aperture settings and shutter speed, a tripod, a photo editing program and a couple of ordinary reading lamps for lighting. Masking, correcting colours, correcting exposure, and so on, is easily done in Windows Live Photo Gallery. I never use flash. I use ordinary (halogen) lamps. Always use a very small aperture for as much depth of field (sharpness) as possible. The drawback is of course that you will have a rather long exposure (that's why the tripod) – especially when the light source is weak. I most often photograph indoors (on my workbench) and using f22 which might give me an exposure of 5-10 seconds. (If you are using your phone as a camera, you might have a problem)

If you have some kind of base and a background, it's great. I often use wall decals as backgrounds as well as backgrounds I have painted myself. Especially for dioramas, the background is essential.

*A photo editing program is always useful for adding something to the picture (for example smoke from a burning engine).*
*I also use it for "melting" two pictures together. What I actually do is cloning one part of a picture (for example the model) and places it in another picture. With very little effort, the images can almost always be much better.*

## The "Black 3" of 2./JG27

This is the Bf109 Trop which was transformed into the crashed plane in the previous pages. Not all Bf109 in North Africa was painted light brown, one of them was the "Black 3" of 2./JG27. She started her career in Luftwaffe as part of 2./I./JG3 in Europe, but was transferred to Africa in late 1940. The rare colour photo (to the right) of this aircraft with its ground crew relaxing and playing cards. It shows clearly the unusual camouflage for an aircraft operating in the Libyan Desert.

**It was this picture which gave me the idea to this diorama**

*The picture from 1941*

## The diorama

I would like to recreate the situation in the 1941-picture of "Black 3" in the Libyan Desert.
I used a piece of hardboard for the base and used sand and some pebbles I found in my back yard to cover the surface. The colour of the Libyan Desert was orange. It was not all sand, but also a lot of stones on the desert floor with small bushes growing in between the stones. What I used was the old electric wire trick: Cut a

*The base painted with acrylic paint*

*The Base made with paper Mache*

bit of a lamp cord, twin the thin metal wires into "bushes", spray the result with a dark colour, spray the "bushes" with hairspray and dip them in some green stuff to make leaves (I use Scenic grass)
In the 1941 picture, the crew is playing cards beside fuel barrels and ammo boxes. The barrels are made worn, but not very rusty because the desert is a very dry place. I tried to make the ground crew as shown in the picture from 1941, using figures from different kits and partly scratch build them to make them look like the crew in the old picture. The scale is 1:32

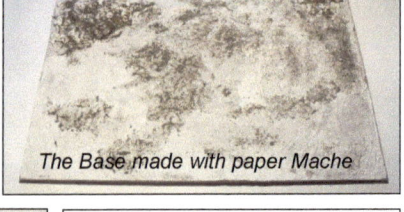

140

## Photographing the aircraft in the air

As I have mentioned earlier: It's always fun to put an aircraft in the air – after all, that's its right element.

I used a photo editing program to do this.
First, I found a suitable backdrop, in this case, a photo of the Sahara Desert. Then I used the photo editing program to «cut» the model out of one of my pictures and paste it on the new background.
The results are often quite amazing:

This is the background photo I used in the picture to the right.
The P-40 was pasted in as a separate operation.
The smoke from the P-40 was made by using the airbrush function in the editing program.

141

# "Kanonenvogel" down

## A Ju87–G is brought down by Soviet AA on the Eastern Front, March 1945

Equipped with a 37mm cannon under each wing, the ageing airframe of the Ju 87 Stuka found new life as an anti-tank aircraft on the Eastern Front in 1943. The "new" Stuka with armour piercing Tungsten carbide ammunition was a deadly weapon to even the heaviest armoured Soviet tanks.
The new design was called the G-model and quickly got the name Kanonenvogel (the CannonBird)

## The Diorama

is a situation at the eastern front in the late winter of 1945. The winter camouflaged Kanonenvogel had attacked columns of Russian tanks and was on its way back to base when it was hit by anti-aircraft shells and the pilot had to make a forced landing in Soviet territory.
He put the plane down on a narrow dirt road, but the terrain was so rough that the starboard main wheel and canon were badly bent before the plane came to a stop.
Unfortunately, the gunner was killed by the AA-shells and the pilot was injured during the landing
Soon after the crash, Soviet soldiers arrived at the site and the pilot was taken prisoner.

The pictures (to the right) of the Ju87-G in the air were made by first photographing the model in the wanted position, then pasting the picture of the plane to the chosen background picture.
This technique is explained several times in this book.

# The Kanonenvogel

I used an old 1/32 model of a plane which I made a couple of years ago (pic right).

All the damages had to be inflicted on this perfectly good model, but that's part of the fun!

So, I was to smash the engine department, the propeller, the port wing, the aft cockpit area, the starboard landing wheel and the cannon pod.

# The Wing

The wing was cut open and ribs (by styrene) placed in the opening together with part of the exposed wing tank made by thin metal sheets.

Thin metal sheets (taken from a tube of bacon cheese) were glued to the opening to make the twisted metal skin of the wing.
Then everything was painted.

# The Engine

The engine was damaged during the crash.
I removed the whole engine department from the plane and glued the visible part of the engine so it could be seen beneath the cowling.
Then everything was glued back on the model - a little twisted and bent.

# The Propeller

The propeller blades were made of wood and splintered during the crash.
The blades were reinforced with metal strips on the leading edge and sometimes the whole length of metal would remain, dangling out from the broken area. I have tried to do exactly that with the blades of this model.

# The Aft Cockpit

The aft cockpit where the gunner was seated was badly damaged. The hood was partly blown away and the fuselage penetrated by shrapnel. This would, unfortunately, kill the gunner who later was dragged out of the cockpit by the Soviet soldiers and put on the ground beside the aircraft.

# The Main Undercarriage

The main undercarriage and wheel on the starboard side were bent and damaged when hitting rocks during the landing.
This was also the case with the gun pod which was partly ripped off but was still hanging under the wing.

*Above is a picture of the same Ju87-model when it was painted in the winter camo, before the crash. This picture is from another setting. This Kanonenvögel belonged to the famous Hans-Ulrich Rudel (see page 68-73)*

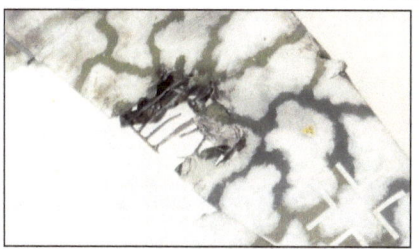

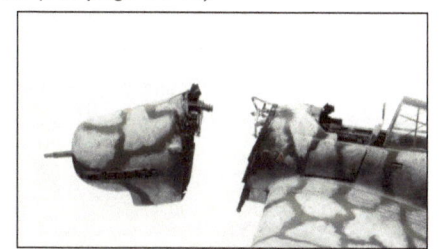

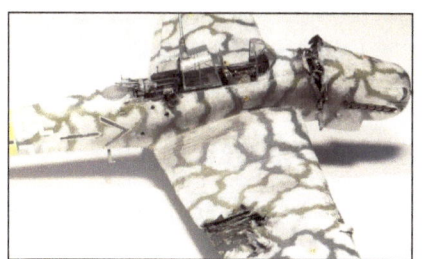

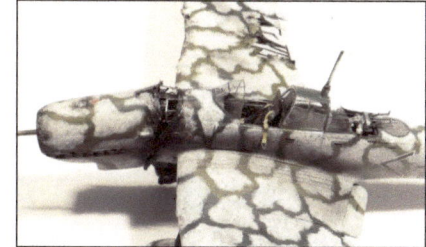

## The Soldiers

The Soviet soldiers and the German crew are scale 1:35
I positioned the soldiers like this: Two soldiers on the wings, looking into the cockpit, one was on his way up on the wing, one was getting the first aid material out of the first aid hatch, one was kneeling beside the dead gunner and the fourth was watching the pilot. The pilot was not badly hurt (although he pretended to be) and later managed to escape from the soldiers finding his way back to the German lines.

## The Base

The base is a 75x50cm (30x20in) plywood plate which I covered with paper Marche and sculpted a dirt road. Some stones from my back yard went into the paper Mache.
After the paper Mache dried, I painted the landscape and the road with acrylic colours and collected some twigs and moss to make the leafless forest which surrounded the dirt road. I also put in two bombs (or artillery) craters for good measure. Last, I added some "Realistic Water" to the road, making it look muddy and wet.

**When everything was put in place,
the Ju87-G Crash-Landing-Diorama looks like this:**

145

146

147

# THE BLACK FRIDAY

## The aerial massacre at the Førde Fjord (Norway) February 9th 1945

This is not an ordinary diorama, but an attempt to make a pictorial story of this incident.

There are three parts in this drama: the Beaufighter TFX heavy fighter, the Mustang escort fighter and the Fw190A-8 Würger. I built all three models, made a background of the fjord and tried to picture the desperate fight between the two adversaries.

### The short version of the story:

On the 9th February 1945, two RAF Beaufighters discovered the German destroyer Z-33 and several other vessels at the outlet of Førde Fjord on the Norwegian west coast.

Even before the two Beaus had returned to base, the planning of an attack had begun and a large strike force of 31 Beaufighters and 12 Mustang escort fighters was assembled.

The plan was to attack the ships out of the fjord and head for the relative safety of the North Sea.

The German, however, was quite familiar with the RAF tactics and had sailed further into the fjord. Here the mountains rise almost vertically from the fjord and it would be very difficult for a plane to hit the vessels with cannon and rockets.

Believing the German destroyer was still at the outlet, the British force started the bomb run deep inside the fjord and was suddenly and unexpected under fire from the German ships almost underneath them.

In February 1945, the famous JG5 Eismeer Geschwader was stationed at Herdla, just outside Bergen and could easily reach Førde Fjord and intercept the Strike Force if alerted in time
They were flying high-performance Focke-Wulfs and most of the pilots were battle-hardened veterans from the northern front, having fought the Russians for over three years.

After the surprise of finding the German ships deep inside the fjord, the Beaufighters had no other choice but to initiate a new attack and they had to get further east to make the attack run out the fjord. The Førde Fjord is about 40km (25miles) long, very narrow in some places and with steep, almost vertical mountain sides.
All this manoeuvring to get in position for a new attack took a long time and suddenly German fighters appeared at the scene.

The JG5 at Herdla had twelve Fw 190 on readiness. They took off immediately when they got the report of the British aircraft.

At Førde Fjord, the first Beaufighter made the attack. Behind him, others were queuing up to make theirs. It was simply not room in the fjord for more than two or three Beaus to attack at the same time.
Projectiles of all calibres were streaming towards the planes from the German ships, making the entire fjord a very dangerous place to be.

Suddenly one of the attacking Beauforts saw a fighter a couple of hundred yards behind and noticed the characteristic broad cowling of a radial-engined Focke-Wulf. Then things happened quickly. Cannon shell exploded and the pilot was seriously wounded. He managed to crash land the plane at the sea and was rescued by civilians and survived.

The 9. Staffel had attacked directly into the swarm of Beaufighters waiting to attack the German ships.

*The pictures above are taken from the Beauforts cannon cameras and show the attack on the German Z-33 Destroyer.*

At about this time the escorting Mustangs discovered the German fighters heading directly towards them and was immediately in aerial combat. The battle soon spread over a large area in all directions. The Beaufighters suffers heavily at the hands of the Focke-Wulfs. Terrified civilians witness how a Beaufighter pursued by a Focke-Wulf was hit several times and crashed into a hillside.
A single Mustang tried to help and attacked the German fighter. An aerial duel developed and the Mustang caught fire and crashed in a pine forest.
Beaufighters were shot down over a wide area and the remaining Beaufighters and Mustangs, many of which were damaged, flew singly or in small groups all the way to Britain. Two damaged Beaufighters had wheels-up landing in the dark. Both crews survived.

## The Aftermath

One Mustang and nine Beaufighters were shot down and 14 young lives were lost and five ended as POW.
The Germans suffered losses too, but not anything like the Allied Force. Two Fw190 was shot down and two German pilots died due to the aerial combat.
In view of the enormous effort and terrible losses, the result of the attack was very disappointing. The Z-33 Destroyer was just lightly damaged and continued its journey to Trondheim.

# No wonder that the RAF later referred to this event as **The Black Friday**

*Most of the following pictures are made by the help of a photo editing program where I pasted different pictures of the model into one picture. An example is the b/w picture on the opposite page. I used a b/w picture of the fjord, pasted two models into the b/w picture and made it all b/w to give it an authentic look.*

149

To make a static diorama of The Black Friday incident is close to impossible.

The scale will be out of any reasonable proportion.

I therefore opted for making the models of the aircraft, painted a background of the fjord and photographed and/or pasted the different actors in a pictorial setting.

On this page, I have photographed the two British aircraft, the Beaufighter and the Mustang.

The only pictures I have arranged are the pictures with more than one of the same aircraft in the air. On these pictures, I photographed the main aircraft against a cloudy background (painted) and pasted the smaller aircraft into the picture later with the same technique I have described several times in this book. The pictures of the aircraft on the ground are photographed with a grassy base and the same cloudy background.

The spinning propellers are done lubricate the propeller shaft and blowing at the propellers with a hair dryer.

150

The two fighters:

**The North American Mustang IV (same as P-51D) and the Fw190 A-8 "Würger"**

The Mustang was one of the best fighters in WWII, but the late models of the Focke-Wulf 190 A-8 Würger was an equal opponent.

The Mustangs dropped their external fuel tanks and went after the Würgers

It is a little strange that the potent Mustangs performed so badly in protecting the Beaufighters against the Focke-Wulfs.

The Germans were actually heavily outnumbered by the Allied aircrafts (even if the Beaufighters were slow, they had an enormous punch in their cannons and machine guns)

Operating at low altitude in a narrow fjord was probably not to the Mustangs advantage and the war hardened pilots in the Eismeer Geschwader did not make the situation easier for the British pilots.

Whatever the reason, the result was disastrous for the Allied Strike Force

The aerial battle took not more than 15 minutes. The result: ten British aiircraft shot down, versus two German

152

*Stringing up the Fw190*

The picture to the left was made by stringing the Fw190 up by thin wires in front of the background. You might see the wires in the picture on top of this page.

I wanted a picture of the air battle and needed the British aircraft in the picture as well. To make a realistic picture, it had to be realistic distances between the aircraft which ment that the two British aircraft had to be downsized compared to the «Würger».
it was not possible to string up the British aircraft together with the Fw190 and take a picture with all three aircraft in the same frame.
I had to take separate pictures of the Beaufort and the Mustang, cut out the models from the pictures and paste them in the Fw190 picture.
The background was painted on a cardboard and show the partly ice-covered fjord and the steep mountainsides. Definitley not the best place to have a dogfight.The smoke from the burning Beaufort and the AA-explosions (from the German ships) were made by using the paintbrush function in the Photo Edit Program

*To the right:
The model of the formidable
Fw190 A-8 «Würger»*

153

# Luftwaffe Graveyard

When the WW2 ended in Europe, what remained of the Luftwaffe in Germany were mostly scattered wrecks and aircraft with empty tanks, unable to take off for the last flight.

In 1945, the raw material situation in Europe was critical. Steel and aluminium in war equipment like aircraft, tanks, ships, helmets, rifles, etc. were a valuable source for production of peaceful products like tractors and kitchen appliances.

The German aircraft were bulldozed in large piles, crushed by tanks, melted and turned into pots and pans or just buried in the ground.

At that time, nobody wanted to see these aircraft in the air again – ever!

## The Diorama

First of all, this was a fine way to get rid of some of my old models. The choice was the trashcan or a diorama.

I chose the diorama and for once, the building of the diorama was very simple.

For the base, I used a base I had used before, so no extra was needed.

The scraped aircraft was already built, just some damages were needed, like removing the canopies, some dents here and a broken wing there – plus all kind of broken parts and rubbish, which I found in my spare part box.

The only model I had to build was the bulldozer (which unfortunately was of Japanese origin, but who cares, a bulldozer is a bulldozer, besides it was the only one available in 1/48).

I also threw in a Jeep and some US soldiers looking for souvenirs in the wrecked aircraft.

Then it was just to put everything on the base, and I had one of the many post-war Luftwaffe graveyards on my work bench!

**A nice way to get rid of old models!**

*Thousands of aircraft, tanks, and all kind of war material was piled up and destroyed after WW2. Not only the German inventory, but even larger numbers of Allied material was sent to the melting pot.*

*Left:
A couple of pictures of the many Luftwaffe Graveyards.*

I am not very good at keeping old models.

For me, the building and the photographing are the most important. Not keeping and dusting.
I usually give my models away, or, more often, just throw them away.
For me, the model building is a hobby, not a lifestyle.
This time I decided to let some of the old models have a new life in a diorama. The diorama was actually very easy and fun to make.
I ripped the models apart and used some of the bits and pieces in my left-over box which usually are full of unused model parts.
Placed on a base, it actually looked like one of the graveyards I have seen on pictures after the war.
The background is a painted cardboard.

To the right:
Some of the models I used and some of the different parts which were spread among and underneath the wrecked aircraft

156

157

# To photograph a model in the air in front of a backdrop

There are several ways of placing a model in the air in front of a background.
Many years ago, I started by stringing the plane up by "invisible" lines (i.e. fishing lines) in front of the background.
It worked OK but it was always a hazard to rig a stand for the lines. It was also hard to get the background right because I either had to paint the background (on a cardboard) or use a printed picture big enough to cover the whole backdrop.

Then I discovered the photo editing programs which can be used for placing the model on all kind of backgrounds. It was easy and the result looked very good.
To impose a model on a background, you need the following:
A background of your choice. You can use your own photos or you can copy one from the net (beware of copyrights).
You need to take a photograph of your model in a position that matches the background.
Now, you have to paste the picture of the model on the background, but only the model, nothing else that might be on that picture.
For this, you need a photo editing program which allows you to "cut out" the picture of the model and to place it into another picture (the background)

There are several Photo Editing Software available, and not all are expensive.
You have to check that the one you choose has the features you want (I use PaintShop Pro). When you learn the technique, it is really easy to make a nice presentation of your model.

As I have said many times: a workbench or a kitchen table as background, never will give your model a fair presentation.

One thing you must bear in mind is that many of the pictures you find on the net have a low resolution.
If you have a high-resolution picture of the model, you either have to resize the background to a higher resolution, or low-size the picture of the model.

The best is to use two pictures of about the same size (resolution).
Often you need to adjust or change the background to make it more suitable for your model prior to the pasting.

For this, you use the same editing program.

*Both the Stuka (including the bomb) and the Thunderbolt was strung up by fishing lines. The backgrounds were large wall decals mounted on cardboards. Rotating propellers are a problem when using fishing lines: the plane will not be motionless when the propellers spins and thus unsharp.*

*On the P-38 picture, I pasted two aircraft (two pictures of the same model) in different sizes and positions. The background was a picture I found on the net. The picture was without explosions so I had to add these before I put the aircraft into the picture.
I found the explosions on the net and pasted these on the train the same way I later pasted the aircraft.
The AAA explosion in the air was made by the airbrush function in the photo program.*

*To the right:
The picture with explosions, but without the aircraft*

*To make the picture of the formation of Super-Flankers (to the left) I photographed the aircraft in three different positions (see below), then pasted the different aircraft separately on a suitable background, tilting the aircraft in the right position and adjusted the aircraft sizes to fit the formation.
The resizing of the models is done at the same time they are pasted on the background.*

*The three stand-alone pictures were used to create the formation picture.*

# The Cobra Manoeuvre

This is an example of pasting a Su-35 model (scale 1:48) and re-arranging the background picture to fit the manoeuvre.

I used the following steps to make this picture:

1. Photograph the model in the right position.
2. "Cut out" the aircraft for pasting
3. Find a suitable background
4. Prepare the background for the model. In this case: using the airbrush function and make the white condensation.
5. Paste the model and adjust the size and tilt to the background

Below are some more samples of pictures where I used the same technique.
As you can see, you can make rather realistic pictures of your models if you want. It is really up to your own creativity!

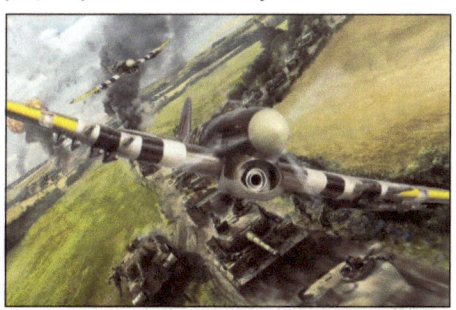

159

# To take pictures of your model

I have seen too many nice models photographed on the workbench, which of course ruins the whole picture and the model does not appear nice. Please don't do that.

A white (or coloured) cardboard (or similar) is a million times better than the workbench—or a kitchen table. Many people believe that the picture taking is very difficult. It isn't, but if you start reading books or look at the net, you will quickly be overwhelmed with technical terminology and apparatuses — and it all seems very difficult.

What you need is a camera which allows you (1) to choose the aperture and (2) adjust to the light (temperature) you are using.

You also need a tripod and a couple of normal reading lamps.

You do not need any flash.

That means most telephones which are used for picture taking are not very suitable for this—a normal camera is much better.

I use an ordinary inexpensive Samsung NX200 with an 18-55mm lens. The aperture should be set to 20 or 22, which often gives a very long exposure (anything from one to twenty seconds is normal).

That's why you need the tripod. The small aperture always gives a long exposure, but also more depth of field, which you need.

For lights, I use normal reading (halogen) lamps. Often two lamps, but sometimes 3 or even 4, depending on how the shadows appear on the model I use. It is important to use lamps with the same colour temperature (same type of light source).

A good advice is to never mix daylight and artificial light. You have to adjust the position and strength of the lights until you are satisfied with the result.

I often need to correct the picture (colour, exposure etc.) and use the Windows Photo Gallery (everyone has this program on their computer).

I will, however, recommend investing in a photo editing program (I use the Corel Paint Shop Pro) for removing unwanted shadows or "stains" or to paste a model into another picture.

There is always something that needed to be corrected when you are taking pictures.

You need the editing program if you want to paste the picture of a model into a certain background picture or if you want to paste several models on the same background. I have given several examples of this in this book. Before I bought the photo editing program, I often used to hang the aircraft in thin fishing threads in front of a background.

That worked fine by the way, but are a little more inconvenient that using a data program.

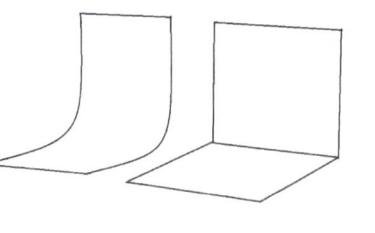

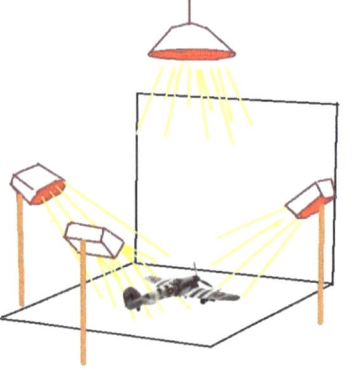

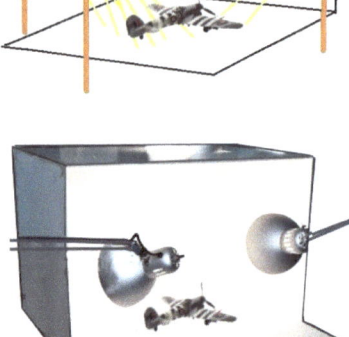

Do not use a glossy background. If you choose to use two separate backgrounds (as I do) at 90 degrees, you risk a dark discoloration in the joint area. The advantage with two white cardboards is that it's easy to set up and stow away.

Anyway, whatever type of background you choose, you need an upper light, which most of us already have.

Then you need at least two light sources (reading lamps will do fine) at each side. If you have a third lamp, that's even better.

Each lamp will cast a shadow and you have to adjust the position and strength of each lamp until you are satisfied with the appearance of the model.

Don't worry if the exposure time is several seconds, the tripod will keep the camera motionless.

And don't use the flash

A photo box (left) is fine for taking pictures of a model, but to photograph a diorama, the box will normally be too small. I prefer the cardboard.

# Scale effect - Adding white to the colours

This has perhaps little to do with building dioramas, but nevertheless, I think it is an important issue. It might be the difference between a model looking like a toy or a scale model.
If you paint a 1/72 model in full strength colour, it will probably not look like a realistic model.
You might have noticed that colours intensity fades the further you get away from the object. If you stand close to an aircraft, the colour might be crisp and strong, but if you see the same aircraft farther away, the colours will be less intense.
The same applies of course to scale models.
If you are viewing a 1/72 aircraft model at 50cm (20in), it is the same as looking at the full-scale aircraft from 36 meters (120ft) away
Of course, it is entirely up to the modeller to decide what to do, but if you want your model to look as «the real thing», you should give the scale effect some thoughts. I have seen plenty of nice models totally ruined by too strong colours
The solution is to add white to almost all the dark colours to reduce the colour intensity
The following is a good a thumb rule:

## 1/72 - add 15% white
## 1/48 - add 10% white
## 1/32 - add 7% white

Beware of the red colour. If you add white, it will turn pink, which is probably not a colour you want to use.
The white colour fades as well, but there is little use of adding more white. Use a little grey instead.
The smaller scale you build (1/300 or 1/700), the more important it is to think about the scale effect. If you build bigger scale (1/24 or 1/32) the scale effect is less important. But of course, I like to emphasise that it's all up to each model maker to decide how to make his model. There are no right or wrong - If you are happy with strong colours, don't let anybody tell you differently.
I am merely pointing out some valid points if your object is to make a time-frame realistic model.

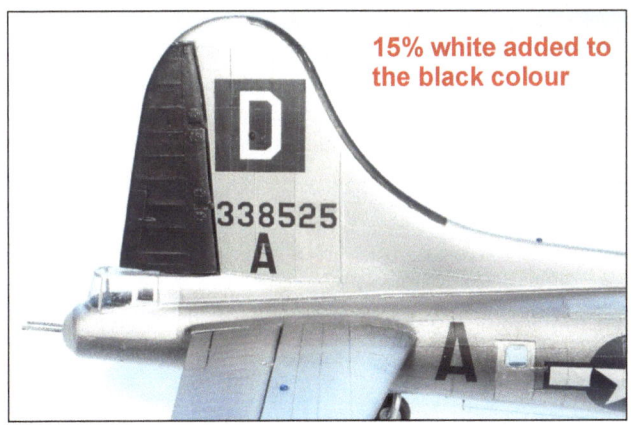

**No white added to the black colour**

**15% white added to the black colour**

*This B-17 tail might be an example.*
*The black in the picture on top might seem nice but is all wrong if the intention is to create a model as close to the real WWII B-17 as possible. Not only is there a scale effect on this 1/48 B-17, but all paints on a B-17 was highly faded because it operated at high altitude and were constantly exposed to high doses of UV lights.*
*The picture underneath is painted with black added 15% white and is far more correct.*

# Making trees and bushes

You will often need bushes and trees in your dioramas. There is a huge selection of trees and bushes which you can buy from your hobby store or on-line. They are all very nice, but they are all very expensive.
If you want to make it yourself, there is an easy and inexpensive way to do it.

A tree or a bush is made by twisting the wires from inside a lamp cord around a wooden stick.

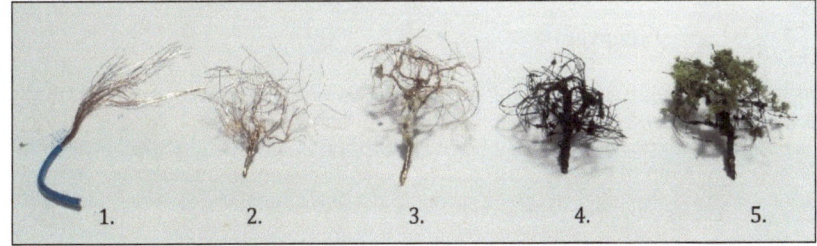

1.   2.   3.   4.   5.

By twisting the wires into smaller parts, it will be branches. By using a thicker wooden stick you can make the tree as big as you want. To get the stem as natural as possible, use clear School Glue, mixed with sawdust. The sawdust is important because it looks like bark on the tree trunk when the glue is dry. How to get sawdust? Find some wood and use a saw. It's that simple.
The stem can be painted by hand, but the small branches should be airbrushed, otherwise, it is almost impossible to paint all the thin wires. To get the leaves on the tree, I sprayed the branches with hairspray and sprinkled it with the artificial grass or something else that look like leaves. It adheres to the hairspray and with a sympathetic look, it could be leaves.
As always, it is only your imagination that limits the creation.
I often use stuff that I find in nature, in most cases, this will be more "natural" than what you can buy and it's free! Of course, the stuff you picked will turn brown in time, but a little paint will often take care of that. Another trick is to soak the leaves in Glycerine - and they will keep the green colour.

# If you are unsure of how to build your first diorama, here are some basic tips:

First, a diorama is a tableau with a motionless group of models or figures representing a scene from a story, from history or from your own fantasy. A plate with a model and a couple of figures is in my opinion not a diorama, but a base for the model.
A diorama should tell a story or be a snapshot of an event, real or imaginary. When you see a diorama, you should immediately understand what's happening, even if you don't know the details of the story behind the work.
All the details in building a diorama will normally develop while you are working, there is no reason to plan everything in detail before you start. The fun is in building and exploring.

The starting point for building a diorama is always the following:

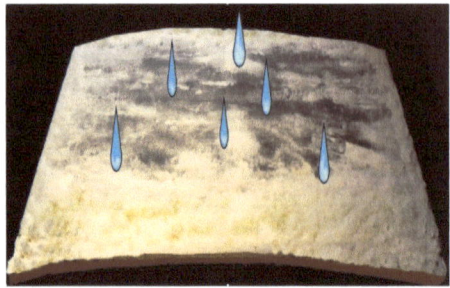

## The Story

The story can have its root in real life, or in your imagination.
It is important to make the story as realistic as possible. That means to think of all the small details which surround us at all times, then try to recreate them the best you can.
This is the most fun: To use your creativity and find solutions to all the small and big problem you must solve. The solution is not to run to the nearest hobby shop to buy all you need, but rather to build or find solutions yourself, often at no cost at all.

## Research

Learn as much as possible about the story or situation you are trying to create. There are always a lot of info on the net – and a lot of pictures.

## Sketch

Make a sketch of the diorama. It's good to have your thoughts down on paper – even if the diorama will develop while you are working on it.

## Models and Base

Decide if you want to start with the model(s) or the base. It's of no consequence, but I always start with the models. The finished models give me a better understanding of how to make the base.
You often have to sculpt the terrain on the base. There are a lot of different stuff you can use to make the terrain: Papier Mache, Plaster of Paris, or if you have some plaster for repairing your home, you can use it as well.
It is of great importance that the base you are building on does not bend when getting wet. This is not a problem with a small base, but if you are making a larger diorama, the bending might ruin the whole base.

## Background

A background is not necessary, but it's always nice to see a diorama where the background gives an extra dimension to the display. You don't have to be an artist to paint a background, especially if you have an airbrush. Light blue, grey and white will often give a good imitation of the sky. But, again, as for the base, the cardboard or whatever you use as a background might bend if it gets wet on only one side. Painting both sides will often take care of the problem.
There are some great wall decals which might be perfect as a background. You'll find some good decals on Amazon or eBay.

## Weathering, Priming, Painting, Mottling, Pre-Shading, Putting, etc

There are a zillion good, (and some not so good) websites, YouTube videos and books taking care of all these issues. There is no reason for me to go into all these subjects.
If there is something you want to learn more about, you will find it on the net.

# What do you need to make your first diorama?

## Honestly, I do not know, because I do not know what you intend to build.

But if I look at what I used to make the dioramas in this book, you'll find most of the stuff I used on this page:

**1.** You need a base. Anything can be a base. But be sure it will stay flat even if it gets wet on one side.

**2.** You need something to mould a terrain. Paper Mache is fine, but any filler or putty you have at home might do nicely

**3.** Sand and small pebbles are always useful in building a terrain.

**4.** If you are building a hilly terrain, some Styrofoam is always handy.

**5.** If you build a creek, a waterhole or an ocean, you need some water. Realistic Water is very useful.

**6.** Some electrical wires if you like to make some trees or bushes.

**7.** Chicken wire if you want some firework

**8.** Cotton for smoke

**9.** Trees and bushes. Bought in a hobby shop or made by you – or picked from your backyard

**10.** The dispenser for making electrostatic grass. Really useful

**11.** Brushes in all sizes.

**12.** Wooden sticks and spatulas. Great for building houses.

**13.** Acrylic paint. The big one you get at the hardware store

**14.** Glue. The ordinary wood glue is most useful

**15.** All the bits and pieces you have in your drawer are useful when building a diorama

**16.** A green carpet can always be turned into a grassy field. Use paint and perhaps a hot iron to get it rough and dirty.

163

# To make an explosion or a fire

In a military diorama, you often want to make fires and explosions.
The most frequent question I get is how to make a realistic explosion or fire.
I know that many want to try this, but are thinking that this is too difficult.

The common fault I see in diorama explosions is too much cotton, too much colour and too little lights.   An explosion is all about lights.

You have seen fire and explosion several places in this book, and here is a summary:

I use the same ingredients in every explosion or fire I have made:

- **Chicken wire**
- **Cotton**
- **Cellophane (sometimes)**
- **LED lights**
- **Airbrush**
- **Hairspray**

## Chicken Wire

The chicken wire is to make a cage around the explosion. This cage is to support the explosion fumes/smoke you want to make around the explosion/fire.

It also helps create a space around the light source which is important for reducing the heat effect from the light.
I use chicken wire because it's very easy to form and very cheap to buy.

## Cotton

The cotton is used to make the expanding gasses from the explosion/fire. I use plain white cotton which is easy to form and can be made bulky or stretched as thin as you like. It all depends on what kind of effect you want to make.

If you want to make the cotton stiff, use a normal hairspray.

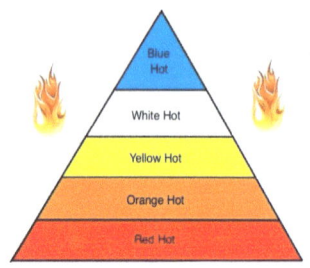

The colour from the light will often be white which might be fine in an explosion.
If you, however, are making a fire, you probably want some yellow and red colours as well.

When an explosive is initiated either to burning or detonation, its energy is released in the form of heat. The colours indicate the heat temperature, from the hottest white/blue to yellow/orange to the warm red colour.

This can be obtained by painting (airbrush) the cotton (i.e. the burning gasses) or/and using coloured cellophane inside the "smoke".
If you are making a fire, you will use black/grey/brown colours, all depending on the situation and the cause of the fire.

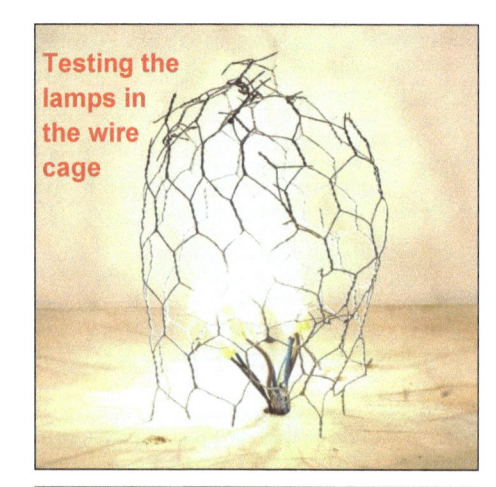

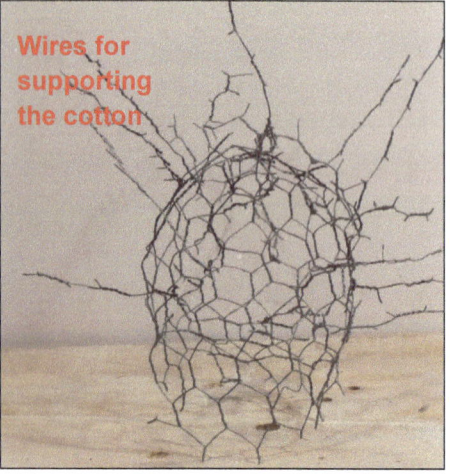

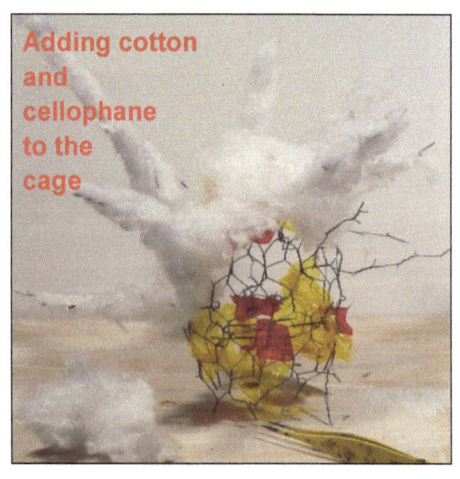

**LED light in place**

**Chicken wire cage**

**Cellophane in cage**

**Cotton on cage**

**Placed in the diorama**

**Testing the lamps in the wire cage**

**Wires for supporting the cotton**

**Adding cotton and cellophane to the cage**

**The explosion in the diorama**

## Light sources

If you are making a fire, an explosion or a rocket launch, you need a light. If not, you have to "paint" the explosion, which more often than not will look as paint and not an explosion.

The lightsource will often be hidden behind smoke or gasses, made by cotton or other flammable material. And that creates a problem: Heat

All lights produce heat when they are lit. And heat may cause the material to melt, to be discoloured or in the worst case to start a real fire.

There are ways to prevent, or at least reduce the chances of this to happen.

The most important is to choose a light that produces as little heat as possible. This sounds easy, but the problem is that you often need a strong light to create the effect you are looking for, and a strong light always produces more heat than a weak light.

The best Lightsource to achieve the effect you want would probably be a LED light. The LED light emits far less heat than for example a halogen light.

Of course, it all depends on how long you want the light to burn each time you turn it on.
If you turn it on only a few seconds each time, you can use any Lightsource you like, but if you want the lights to burn a long time, you must consider the heat effect.

There are large heat differences between different LED lights and you have to try it out before you decide which one to use.

I have used 3W LED lights connected directly to 220V which produces a strong light and very little heat. The most useful LED lights I have used are 12V lights which emit very little heat. I use a 12V transformer connected directly to the outlet (220V or 110V).

One additional advantage with 12V is that you can use very thin wires between the transformer and the lamp(s).
And thin wires are easier to hide than thick wires.

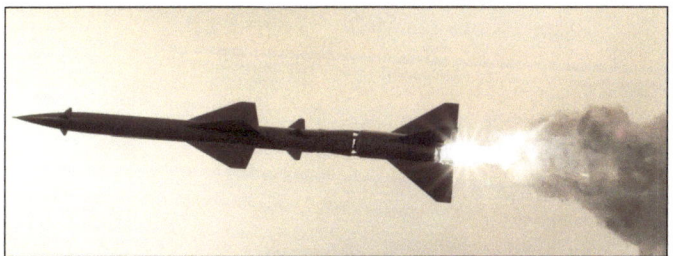

## Airbrush

To paint the cotton, you need an airbrush. Painting by hand is almost impossible. The cotton will be very wet and loose the fluffy texture you need to make smoke

*An explosion is always white at the core and yellow and red at the edges*

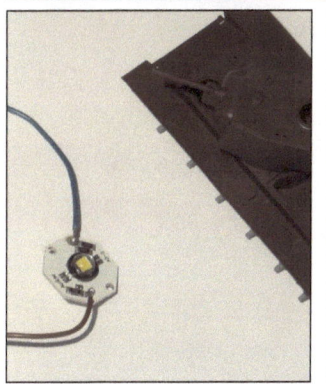

*A 220V 3W LED lamp that emitts very little heat, but gives a bright hvite light*

*Another example of using LED light. The wires are hidden in the smoke*

*Different ways of using LED lamps and airbrushed cotton*

165

If you want more details, more background stories and see more pictures of the different dioramas and models by Bjørn Jacobsen, you can visit the website

**www. dioramas-and-models.com**

167

# British & American English

*It is not easy for one who's native language is Norwegian to write 28.000 words in "English"*

*Especially if you know that about half of the readers will have American as their language while the other half claim British as their native tounge..*

*So, what does a poor sod do when he has to choose between color or colour, aeroplane or airplane, grey or gray, criticise or critizise, modeling or modelling, harbour or harbor, to fill in or to fill out? And so on and so forth.*

*Knowing that whatever I choose, it will be "wrong" and someone will put a red mark in the book indicating a misspelling.*

*I did the only thing I could do, I wrote this book in the "English" I felt was natural for me and ask you not to feel too strongly about the British/American language soup (or any other spelling soup) I am making.*

*Bjørn Jacobsen*

a language frustrated Author (Writer)